Broken English

ENGLISH

BROKEN

Poetry
and
Partiality

Heather
McHugh

Wesleyan University Press

Published by

University Press of New England

Hanover and London

Wesleyan University Press

Published by University Press of New England, Hanover, NH 03755

Printed in the United States of America   5   4   3   2   1

CIP data appear at the end of the book

Selections from *Poems of Paul Celan* translated by Michael Hamburger. Copyright © 1972, 1980, 1988 by Michael Hamburger. Reprinted by permission of Persea Books, Inc.

"The Course of a Particular" is reprinted from *Opus Posthumous* by Wallace Stevens. Copyright 1957 by Elsie Stevens and Holly Stevens. Reprinted by permission of Alfred A. Knopf, Inc., and Faber and Faber Ltd.

Contents

Prefatory Note

Most of these essays were delivered as lectures at the MFA Program for Writers at Warren Wilson College in Swannanoa, N.C., and as Elliston Lectures at the University of Cincinnati.

Several appeared in the *American Poetry Review*, and "A Genuine Article" appeared in *ZYZZYVA*. I'm grateful to Cornell Capa and Magnum Photos for the chance to reprint the Robert Capa diptych here. Ulli Beier's work was my first and best resource for the Yoruba piece. Indeed at every turn I relied on good works already done: Ed Snow's translations of Rilke, the editions of Valéry in the Bollingen Series, the sensitive translations of Celan available to us through Michael Hamburger and Katharine Washburn, Guy Davenport's Archilochus, Stanley Lombardo's Parmenides and Empedocles, and more. Tom Phillips's treated texts deserve especially warm mention.

I thank the Creative Writing Program and English Department of the University of Washington in Seattle, for ungrudging grants of leave, during which some of these essays were written and revised; the Guggenheim Foundation, for support during one year of the writing of these essays; and the Coal-Royalty endowment at the University of Alabama, for the award of a Chair which gave me relief from teaching and time to write.

From the encouraging response of people who heard these lectures, or who read the essays in advance, came my determination to collect and finish them. But to my hardest critic and best friend, I owe most of all: Niko Boris McHugh, whose erudition kept me honest, and whose constancy kept me whole. It is to his high standards and intellectual integrity that I owe any refinement this book possesses; its immoderacies are mine.

Introduction

I have not extirpated all sentimental attachment from my affections, God help me. Right now mine tend to collect with lapidary precision around a particular spot on earth, 45 degrees latitude, 67 degrees longitude, where all the addresses end with a ME and an US.

But it is not THAT sense of place, the place of sentimental attachments, the place of literal topographies, I hold poetry answerable to. To be frank, the inevitable panel discussion on the "poetry of place" bores me: it takes place too literally.

Poems take place as time takes it; and they address their object as an attention does. The place of poetry is nothing less than the place of love, for language; the place of shifting ground, for human song; the place of the made, for the moving. Like other loves it cannot be free of the terrible; it is barely dictable at times, certainly not predictable. It verges on (and toward, at last) the unsayable, even the unspeakable. The place of the poem is the place of our homelessness, our groundlessness. A poem is untoward.

In the field of positions, a passionate position is like a held fire. Robert Creeley opens "The Window" with the line "Position is where you put it . . ." Given the fire of language, *ex*position is (etymologically speaking) where you put it *out*.

Exposition means to mean, mainly. Its language intends to dissolve in the service of its meaning. Exposition's means is its invisibility: it aims elsewhere; you look through it at its object. Exposition is a very windexed window.

It is not itself the place where its ends are inscribed: its means mean nothing, next to its ends. It does not give itself as evidence, as inscription (or conscription); at its closest to its object, it offers *de*scription.

That is why poetry is not exposition. It *is* the place that suffers inscription. It bears the mark or scar of what was seen and what was grasped. Its hand is script (felt, hammered, or quilled). Its eye cannot disappear in service: it fills with shades and shines. Everything moves in it (as everything moves in the mind); its glass is not transparent but is the sign of the seer's own slant. It takes upon itself, into itself, what it sees; the song is of insight. Whether out of joy or grief, it sings us in, and as it does, we are moved—from explication to implication, from ex- to im-position.

For poetry is imposition and self-exposure, urgency and deferral. Its act is tenacious: and its hold can hurt. In me, that hurting place is locable moreorless where God used to be; but you must remember how illocable that is.

The window of Creeley's "The Window" is a place where we hold the world, a place where we take in what took us in. It is a window that can weep (it's an eye), a window that can be beaten (it's a heart); it is a changeable, a perishable place. Poetry isn't made to make you forget the insecurity of its status, or our own: it is not for burying the terror, salving the sorrow, buying a balm. No salesman's music or easy analgesic, it is not in the comforter business. For its regards are not formalities: they require us to notice what we might otherwise most wish to overlook. Imagination isn't needed, says Valéry, to see what isn't; it is needed to see what *is*. That's what we most deeply miss.

The position of poetry is THAT imposition: it requires you to face the difficulty, the unfathomability, of your life. When Rilke writes "You must change . . . ," you feel the force of that embrace. It's merciless. Says Creeley, "I can feel my eye breaking." That brokenness, the broken regard in which we hold all being, that is poetry's place.

II. The Part of Poetry

The poem is a space of time. In it occur patterns for eye and ear, our curious catchers of frequencies. To my eye and my ear, the poem has always been a graphicality and score; and to my mind, mind's meat.

I notice patterns—it's my habit as a poet, as a reader, as a student of phenomena, as a sensual being in nature. In this sense, my work as a writer and my work as a reader are similar: I study and then remark patterns: occurrences, recurrences, currents.

When I call poetry a form of partiality, I mean its economies operate by powers of intimation: glimmering and glints, rather than exhaustible sums. It is a broken language from the beginning, brimming with non-words: all that white welled up to keep the line from surrendering to the margin; all that quiet, to keep the musics marked. The frame of the still photograph, and its eventualities in time, are a poetic frame.

The poem occurs in an old time (the undone) and in an old language (the penultimate). It contradicts itself, is true twice. The forked tongue, second face, double bind got bad press: everyone's from two. And poetry is of two minds: it is language's way of being of two minds.

That is why I say it's broken language. In poetry, by definition, the making of lines is the breaking of lines (in this way poetry's deeply unlike prose, the units of which are sentences, defined grammatically by their completeness). Poetic language is language in which meaning refuses to be single-minded: the transitivity of meaning splits, as we mean more than we intend. More like evidence than judgment, the well-crafted poem can present several versions at once; it is the site of possibility. Having so many ends, it remains open-ended.

In very literal ways, the fragment essay included in this book considers the implications of broken language, and queries the idea of the whole (an idea always just behind the thought of fragments).

But some of the richest constructions were always the sparest. That is how Dickinson and Celan both amaze me. Their lyricisms are fuller for the spaces, their structures a math of the missing: no load of cogito sum but something more like light—reducible neither to wave nor to particle, yet somehow irreconcilably each, irrefutably both.

It is the space that defines the words, the skull the kiss, the hole the eye. Among the essays collected here are one paying homage to the way silence deepens around Celan's language until we feel how life itself is only briefly spared. One essay is an appreciation of Dickinson's characteristically terse structures, which generate so many mutually resistant yet simultaneous readings. (How much smaller would her sums have been, if all their plusses and equals had been signed, as her first and tidiest editors wished, making her more accessible, assessable, and smug.)

One piece is a reading of the photographic diptych "Tour de France" (that circle of circles, seen through two squares); and one is a piece on pieces, taking for its occasion the artistic fragment, both archaic and (as *garde* will go) *avant*. There is a little theme and variations on *a* and *the*:

attention to the differing integrities of grammatical articles (the definite's presumptions, an indefinite's permissions). There is an admirer's inquiry into works of Rilke and of Valéry, whose fluidities of sense greaten the senses of meaning. Through Rilke we can learn to attend, rather than intend, what we mean; of Valéry it seems true, as Emilie Teste said of her husband, that "his eyes are a little larger than visible things."

For it is not that the eye (or the first person singular either) *holds* the whole; rather, it sees how deep things are, and sees no end of things. (No infinity but in finity!) Finally there is a celebration of the work of translator Ulli Beier, who studied Yoruba songs, their premises in no detention. Even in our ignorance (of the shadings of drum-language, nature of praise-naming) American poets can close-read these transcriptions to advantage; salutary cautions and encouragements abound.

I am interested in ways language can suggest or provoke (though never surround) an endlessness. Exclusionary practica of meaning, no less than convictions of the whole as sayable, seem to me to impoverish poetic means. I mean to think of partiality as something greater, paradoxically, than comprehending. For a whole (which is a sack of intent) is too tidy, too bounded, for the extent, the portent, the attent, of the poetic . . .

Poetry is a declared partiality, a love *of* (not entirely *in*) words. The line is by definition broken. If you yearn for wholeness, maybe you need fiction. Unadulterated feeling is a freak of reason or intent: in the chemistries of real life, feelings are always being mixed. How to set off the reaction in the reader—with its whiffs of the ineffable, its shifts of solubility, its dusts and distillates? The work of poetry, the poet's work, takes its place in the reader.

The poet works by feel for the physical materials of language, and by dint of sympathy. Poetry is a discipline of attention: we must not just re-use but re-materialize the language; no old saw may go unsharpened, no old privilege be presumed. For nothing is foregone, for poetry; instead, everything is gone, again and again: at the end of each line another nothing.

So there was never only one nothing, never only one everything. The poem keeps recasting those unlimiteds. It is a framer's art, and the frame is a part (not apart), a way (not away). With great care, not only the poem but the line, not only the line but the word, and not only the word but the letter, can remind us of the space in which they rest. Recalled to our attention is the very medium of media: all those deepening split-seconds we spend decades (glib, or destination-greedy) missing. The poem trips us up. The trippage, the breakage, is not only how, but what, its metric means. There is no of-course about it, and (in its course) no end of ends.

The Store

*

W e come to acts of experience, in particular to acts of art, with a store of unexamined premises—the operative features of time and space among them. At the moment we speak of a present, we create a past. ("Just now," says an American, and means a certain moment in the past.) In the very act of language we incur the language's forethought and afterthought; and generally, to that extent, we abrogate for ourselves an independent or unpredictable present.

As a grammatical category, that is, as a taxonomic entity, the present operates as a range within the temporal field: accorded for its operations one third of the stretch, it works like the past and future, and is distinguished from them only by its operations' imputed location-in-time. But even as we say it, we know a greater mystery is involved.

For the future feels inherently unpredictable to us; that unforeseenness is its essential incommensurability with the past, in this triad of wrongly-parallelized constructs. The present extends not even a split-second backward or a split-second forward, and has the feel of a constantly slipping location. It is enormous (we can never get out of it) and yet tiny (it can't for a second keep from becoming past) and seems, at times, to mark only the—split—border between past and future, and not a separate range at all. The space of time is thus, as phenomenal experience, suggestive of a very different kind of construction, with none of the divisibility or structural equitability of the tidy grammatical fields.[1]

For the writer, as for the photographer, the paradox of the attempt to capture the Now arises immediately and pointedly. In many ways, the best definition of art is that it raises this paradox to view, that it offers to the looker (the audience) the prospect of another looker (the artist) whose presence is both gone and going-on. The "store" which I take for my title here is, first and foremost, that store or warehouse of prescriptions or recapitulations we bring to the experience of a moment. For the present is both a monumental moment (from which we get the sense of the momentous) and a molten flow or constant loss, which breaks down unities and gives us the nomenclatures of seconds, always already split.

Though we sense these paradoxes, now and then, and must face them in the moment in the act of art, we operate as a practical matter in the world as if looking forward were symmetrical with looking back; we frame the moment in the economies and containabilities of the grammatical taxonomy, and forget we've framed our way of seeing, framing (as we do) some possibilities out. For all our wish to cover and recover in language everything we experience, still it turns out what's missing isn't nothing (we've covered nothing, too): something, not nothing, is missing in the way we see.

Asked where endlessness is located, what the realm or home of endlessness might be—the visible or the invisible—most of us would locate endlessness in the unseen; we'd do, that is, what we did as children, populate eternity with ghosts and say the sensible has the natural limits. But it is exactly that presumption, that prejudice, that blinds us. We cannot see all of the visible, ever; that is where the ache of the endless is greatest; we can't say all we do see, and, worst of all (because it needn't be) we're always missing much of what's in front of us, under our noses, before our eyes.

Our mythographies have always placed the past behind us, and reserved the space ahead for the future. I always loved the reminder that in some mythographies the past is construed to be ahead, where it's visible, and the future behind us, since it can't be seen. Such variances in the visualization of temporal space serve to remind us, with a shock of recognition, of the underlying power of our own fictions of construction. When Picasso says his object isn't what he's looking for, we have to rethrow our thinking about the jectified (*jacere* meant to throw, from the first). When Rilke studies a ball in air, he observes how it throws its handlers; when Robert Capa watches the watchers at an event, he sees subject and object not bordering but abounding-in each other. In studying a few pieces by these two, the poet Rilke[2] and the photographer Capa,[3] I mean to consider what we *hold in mind* as mind moves over the landscape of an artwork; whether there is a stillness or *idée fixe* in the store of concepts we bring to moving experience; how the work of art refocuses our attention on our stillings (instillings, distillings) while moving us; and how the turns of the artistic moment replace the elements in a presumptive critical arrangement—unpacking what is stored in the way we look and locate, recovering for the reserved space or premises of time a certain illocability, and re-storing to the present (to the *seeable*, that is) its real topos and subject, the *unseen*.

*

Robert Capa's photographic diptych "Tour de France" is also a *tour d'adresse* or sleight of hand, for it shows not the athletes we'd ordinarily consider to *be* the event, but rather two views of one row of bystanders or onlookers, occupying two moments one might call before and after the "event" (the bicyclists' passing). We see the onlookers framing the event, looking forward and then looking afterward, in space and time, transitive and intransitive, turning (in a nice turn on the French *tour*) from anticipators to aftergazers.

The racers, the eponymous topic of the diptych, are *present* only as sketched in the figures that, craning, foresee and then, crouching, recall them. The onlookers become the language in which the event is transcribed for us, the second rank of onlookers, because superficially missing is something most conventionally central in our store of ideas about art: its subject.

What is *still* photography's relation to events in time? Whenever it addresses its object directly, it seizes it out of relation-in-time, it holds what was not holdable, it gives us time to study what in the usual stream of changes we could miss, but also it robs the studied object of change, in which it lived. (Even the high-jumper's foot was not in air, as it would be on the page, so long, and the quality of the beloved's smile was in its waver, not its photo-fixity.) By displacing the camera's attention to the onlookers, Capa reminds us that the looking itself is his subject, and reminds us of the mind's takes (and mistakes) on things. Art takes for holdable what in experience will not stay put; and only to the extent that the artist confesses this violation (this fundamental failure of the represented to be the present, exactly because it adds a re- and an -ed to the present), only by keeping the infidelity to some degree his subject, does the artist suggest the depth of his understanding and of our quandary.

Tour de France, Pleyben, Brittany, July 1939. Photo by Robert Capa. Permission granted by Magnum Photos, Inc.

Tour de France, Pleyben, Brittany, July 1939. Photo by Robert Capa. Permission granted by Magnum Photos, Inc.

Ambrose Bierce sorrowfully observed, the trouble with mind is it's all we have to study mind with. The perennial problem of our being sunk in our limiting perspectives is engaged (if not escaped) when the limitation itself is taken for object.

The problem of the subject is also, structurally, the problem of language. The subject of experience is the experiencer, but the subject of an essay is its object. The semantic difficulty goes deep, because subject and object are so hard to disentangle, even once one stabilizes one's philosophical terms. The point of the Capa perspective branches into dilemma: in making the audience his object, he directs our attention not only toward the missing object (the bicyclists toward whom THEIR attention is turned) but toward the missing subject: the viewers *of* the viewers, the audience we are, who gaze toward and back on the French crowd. We, with the photographer, establish other presents from which the act of audience can be regarded. Thinking spatially of the spectacle at issue, we are located vis à vis the crowd, where the race must have been when it was present in front of them. Looked at as seers, we take on the position of the (vanished) seen. At the moments these two photographs were taken, the race was not directly in front of the crowd, but the photographer was. By virtue of his intervention, we (the second audience) establish another before- and aftermath. These perplexities of subject and object, presence and disappearance, call our attention to the question of what it means to *be* vis à vis the artistic event or object.

In the unmarked field existing between us and the artist, other paradoxes crop up. In this nest of con- and de-centricities, this riddle of seers and scenes, is the photographer to be imagined as before or behind us? In this case the opposite of before isn't behind, most accurately, but after, since if he were before us in space, we'd see him, and if he were behind us in space, he'd more literally see us; the very thought of the photographer requires us to construct in our minds the probable scene on the near side of the street—another line of lookers, foremost among whom is the man with the camera. But the fiction of photography is the fiction of identity: we enter into a contract of faith through which we are an other; we see things through his eye and stand in his place. Time, rather than space, separates us most from the artist, and the circle this "tour" de France portrays is temporal as much as spatial. (In a sense, it is a portrait of the France that watches the races, invests so much of itself in them, and turns itself to them; it is, in other words, a picture of the "turning of France" to the Tour de France.)

The artist "in" his work raises the paradoxical figure of a past that is in front of us. The artist's operation projected us in relation to its object;

it foresees our act of seeing. We *are* the audience which is this diptych's object and yet we are outside it; we bear the relation to audience that we bear to language: we stand as if outside it to describe or define it, even to speak of it at all; and yet we can't escape the fact we're always speaking *in* it, when we speak. By definition, in watching the watchers, we watch what we are. Making use of photography's characteristic drawback to reach us over the otherwise unbridgeable time-chasm, the photographer is out to get us (he is not only before us, but after us). Seeing is always going on, but by virtue of the still photograph, looking can stay awhile. And how we look is, after all, part of the spectacle's auspices, in the artist's eye: the future foreseen, the past looked after.

*

In the swirl of meanings of "subject" at issue in this Capa diptych, the conventionally primary one (the topic, the nominal performers of the "event," the content of the piece as titled) is left out of the visual field. The bicyclists themselves, unmarked, are not however unremarked. Indeed, their having-been-there has left its traces not only in the slight wind of their aftermath (look at the newspaper held by a spectator!—events do leave their ring signatures, their eddies and wakes) but also in the excited postures of the lookers bent to what they've seen. Look at the boy whose sympathy turns his whole body, after his heroes have passed, toward the posture of a bicyclist. For it is their future that children are always practicing, and what has just passed in the form of a bicyclist is this child's image of his future, for the moment (the word *ambition*, too, has its etymological go-around in it). To judge by these two photographic shots, not only in retrospect but in anticipation, too, do events inscribe themselves. Every object has a field of force (you could say it is the event-ual field) affecting other objects (and subjects) from afar. Rilke's poem "The Ball" plays with such "*actio in distans*"; for the object of concentrated attention is not only invested, but invests again the ones around it, with responsible gesture. Here object partakes of event, and rearranges its subjects in forecast and consequence.

The Ball

You round one, who take the warmth from two hands
and pass it on in flight, above, blithely
as if it were your own; what's too unburdened
to remain in objects, not thing enough

and yet sufficiently a thing so that
it doesn't slip from all the outer grids

and glide invisibly into our being;
it glided into you, you between fall and flight

still the undecided: who, when you rise,
as if you had drawn it up with you,
abduct and liberate the throw—, and bend
and pause and suddenly from above
show those playing a new place,
arranging them as for a dance's turn,

in order then, awaited and desired by all,
swift, simple, artless, completely nature,
to fall into the cup of upstretched hands.

The poem interests me (as do so many of Rilke's poems) as a physical (object) study that turns into a metaphysical (subject) study. The last line's "fall into the cup of upstretched hands" suggests nothing so much as the answer to a prayer: but the answer is a downfall, back into the realm of earthly bonds; the answer is "completely nature." Rilke's desire for an answer is also the desire (invested in the poem as metaphor) that the analogy overcome the difference between the physical throw (of a thing) and the intentional one (of a verbal construct: a prayer, a poem). Insofar as the poem is his sport, he thus secures the return, the reception, the touchdown, if you will. But insofar as it is spiritual yearning, I'm convinced that the suspension of the object in space, the pausing of the poem in that long (endless) moment between inclinations (past and future, "had drawn" and "to fall"), amounts to an example of spiritual presence: neither rising nor falling, bound by neither past nor future, being, like a point, dimensionless.

The ball will, we are assured, as "desired by all," fall back into the cup of forces and uses. The answer in this case is "completely nature," and this is Rilke's characteristic spiritual insistence: that animation rises out of (and will, we are sure, fall back into) nature. To the human underling, the inclination that is "too unburdened to remain in objects" looks rather like the sign of transcendental promise—but falls back, *as* a sphere of natural law, into the sphere of natural law, to be the answer to the "upstretched hands." The answer to the praying hands is what was in them in the first place. But for the long moment of the poem, in a suspension of deepening disbelief (subjective genitive!), the object seems to have escaped the forces of our plans and planet.

The trail of gestures in the poem is worth tracking. First, motion itself seems to be drawn from people into the object of their attentions (Rilke calls this motion "warmth"; I call it "animation"; one could call it "life"—in which case the poem investigates the question of what we do with life, where we locate it, where it goes). Then the gesture in which the motion originated is "abducted and liberated" from its physical origins (this phase has its counterpart in the Capa after-photo, where a sympathy of gesture is swirled into the bystander—or swirled from him—by the bypassers). This is the moment in which the seers are themselves shaped by the seen, the maker by the made. The object's uncatchability is dwelled on, not its catchability; what the artistic gesture frames is, at the same time, unlimited. The poem moves into the present's stillness, a moment in which it has arranged its subjects, and thus set up about it what will persist as tracery. In Rilke it is the moment when, at its height, the ball arranges its catchers; they seem *thrown under* it, at that turn, rather than it thrown over them—a turn or *tour de force* of etymological project, disposing subject and object nicely in its field. The object will answer the subject's yearning by returning (bound from boundless) into grasp, but the poem persists in the moment of ungraspability.

The bicyclists, the putative object of the Capa photograph, are missing but have been framed by their viewers or subjects, who then become our object. We find ourselves in the position of the artist looking at people who are looking toward and after what will never be (for us) in sight, and is only fleetingly in sight for them. In time, the greater event comprises the eponymous event's anticipation, its perception, and its memory, and these parts indeed replace each other, successively, so that even within one viewer what is perceived changes as memory performs its operations on it. And several viewers will all remember differently in any case: this one's experience had the feather of a hat bobbing in and out of it, that one felt heartburn at the edges of the perceptual field, this one once had ridden bicycles himself in competition and so noticed details of style and equipment that had changed since his day; and so forth down the line of onlookers. The instability of the nominal "event" is part of what we see in the de-tour Capa inscribes in the space where we expected the "Tour" to be.

Absent are both the innermost object and the outermost subject from the photographic range. (That is, both the bicyclists, moved and re-moved, and ourselves, moved and removed, who, as we look at the photo-graph, form the outermost circle of onlookers, outliving even the pho-tographer himself.) Yet both the bicyclists and ourselves are powerfully evoked in the radiations of subject around object, object around object, subject around subject. We are thrown beyond ourselves like Rilke's ges-tural object, thrown out of the intender's will and into the future tense's will.

The bicyclists are thrown not only past but into their onlookers through gesture, and the boy's body catches the bicyclist's posture. And this is how a self is thrown into us, or we into a self—subject into object, back into forth, up into down, our being is, like language, as much nominal as verbal, as much gesture as thing, as much thrower as thrown, and as much unfixed in time as illocable in space. Art, producing nominally fixed things, must somehow intimate that other nature, which is motion's, casting sub- and ob- ject back and forth into relation.

This is the true thrust, I think, of Rilke's famous "Archaic Torso of Apollo":

> We never knew his head and all the light
> that ripened in his fabled eyes. But
> his torso still glows like a candelabra,
> in which his gazing, turned down low,
>
> holds fast and shines. Otherwise the surge
> of the breast could not blind you, nor a smile
> run through the slight twist of the loins
> toward the center where procreation thrived.
>
> Otherwise this stone would stand deformed and curt
> under the shoulders' invisible plunge
> and not glisten just like wild beasts' fur;
>
> and not burst forth from all its contours
> like a star: for there is no place
> that does not see you. You must change your life.

What *we* cannot see is very much the point here, not what the eyeless figure cannot see. The conventional locus of portraiture, the conventional object (that is, the figure's head and eyes) are missing. But seeing enters the seen everywhere, and this is the thrust of art and the thrust of the idea of god. Two seers or three are immediately evoked—the god, the artist, and ourselves. In the religious as well as the artistic mystery, the part becomes whole only insofar as what exceeds it enters it. In a way, the poem offers the statue, in a brilliant synechdochic move, as emblemmatic of the part entered by the whole: the human body (partial as truncated stone) occupied by (impartial) spirit. It glows, it moves in turns, it is furred with feeling. Exactly to the degree that life has entered this stone, in an act of art or grace, spirit enters us. Where we thought to find only broken stone (figure for ourselves without animation of spirit) there turns out to be starlight and animal elegance—attributes we'd have placed on the one hand above, on the other below, us. (Is the god's "fur" there to remind us of the "uncontrollable mystery on the bestial floor," as Yeats puts it?) We're never unaware, in Rilke, that the greatened gaze may be an unbearable one: we are perhaps creatures made only for slant truths and gradual dazzlements. But though it may not comprehend, it can (itself) shine; and the human form itself, inhabited by greatened gaze, turns out to be a compound of inseparable orders of star and wild animal, features visible in this act of art. And we spectators, unless we have a greatened gaze in us, turn out (despite our having heads and eyes) to have been blind.

Most contemporary American poets I've talked to interpret the poem as culminating in an ethical promise—that is, in the command to reunderstand or reanimate one's life under that gaze, the gaze of fulfilled spirit in abbreviated body, its life extending beyond the limits of corporeal outline. But there is a bleaker view to be considered. One can understand the last line's "must" in a more threatening light—more a foreshadowing of necessity than an opportunity for will. Then it seems to require of us what we *cannot* choose or would not choose, insisting on fatality not freedom. In this reading, the "change" is not *in* life but *of* it: you must die, in other words, and thus change your life. This message would be the *memento* from the god (who looks like mere matter) that you are yourself only matter that looks, for a while, like a god. This bleaker reading, though less palatable to a solution-loving, heaven-craving, optimistic cultural taste, rather resembles the Nietzschean disciplines and severities of the Rilke who chose to record really horrifying realities in the object-studies of 1907 and 1908. Look at poems like "The Stylite" and "Corpse-Washing" in the *New Poems*, and you'll see how fiercely stripped of comfort he has trained his eye to be. Or take a poem like "The Beggars," to understand how thorough-going is Rilke's intention to study, not to avert his gaze from what might otherwise repel us, looking the object into some kind of subject-hood.

The Beggars

You didn't know what the heap
was made of. A foreigner found
beggars in it. They sell
the hollows from their hands.

They show the one who's journeyed here
their mouths full of muck,
and he may (he can afford it)
see how their leprosy eats.

In their weirdly devastated
eyes, his foreign face starts melting;
and they exult in his downfall
and spit when he speaks.

The poem is merciless in its description of the encounter between what we might take to be a (well-fed?) tourist and a huddle of beggars whose flesh itself is eaten away by disease. The brilliant interpenetration of conditions—the one who can eat, the one who is eaten; the one who can pay to "see how their leprosy eats," the one whose poverty is all he has on hand to sell; the mouth that speaks, matched (or challenged—Rilke keeps it perfectly undecidable) by the mouth that spits—all of this reiterates the savage vacancy in the premises of flesh. A nothing with holes in it—that is the view of the human body. The dichotomy suggested between foreigner and natives is complicated by the lepers' "native" human estrangement: ostracized in all societies, their privilege as "natives" soon dissolves into their status as the ostracized; so each (self) in the poem is marked by otherness, with no non-other that could stand his own ground. "Natives" and foreigner enter into a kind of moral exchange, in which the former sing for their supper (that is, they beg: they open their mouths and the eaten-away mouth becomes, itself, the claim on the benefactor's mercy) and he pays for the trouble and insult they represent, the trouble and insult carnal suffering must enact on the human body. If their eyes leak, then he melts in their eyes; the melting is both a figure for his pity, and the hard evidence of their condition; if they spit, it is perhaps the only speaking available to a torn mouth; but he can't be sure they don't disdain him too, who stoops to distinguish himself from them, whose dropped coin can only redescribe the distance between them, and the direction down. The distaste is plainly recorded. Rilke doesn't flinch from the cruelest possibility: that the gesture we'd most love to read as pity's boon and virtue's gift might also re-poison the relationship; that his gesture might only reinscribe his altitude, that neither party might act in generosity. He won't give until he sees how low they are, and they might wish of him a downfall (not only in coin but his own come-down).

The circles of zeroing, in relationships in this poem (starting with the odd and never-again-mentioned pronoun, whose very presence, at the outset, suggests an absent "I" who'd so address a "you") include visual circles of ciphers or vacancy—frustrating attempts to corral a value. The heap becomes people, but only when the foreigner comes by; the hands have something to sell: holes or hollows, the space where something should be. The bodies of the beggars are a patchwork of paucities—first with no life in them (the heap), then with hollows for hands, then with mouths full—but of muck (their disease eats them, and the muck may be the rot flesh itself falls into: here the line between the familiar and the alien is again transgressed, just as disturbingly as it was when the heap first turned out to be human). The benefactor falls into their eyes and in their eyes his face too gets distorted; the last line's alliterative sputtering ("and spit when he speaks" / "*und speien, wenn er spricht*") makes the beg-

gar and the bestower resemble each other, so speech is only a spitting, or
spitting is only a speaking. Still, at some level we reserve a suspicion the
exchange may be perversely conservative of their difference, whether or
not to speak patronizingly was his fortune, or to spit without malice their
misfortune.

There is a kind of twist of opposition-in-identity at work here as elsewhere in Rilke. In this poem it equally creates nothing-out-of-something,
and something-out-of-nothing, at every level. One feels it at issue in
opposition and resemblance, presence and absence, subject turned object
—and the essentially Rilkean uncontainability of being, whether in the
truncated torso of stone or the oozing face of leprosy. And there is always
the challenge to art itself in these constructions; for the question arises
whether the speaking imitates or provokes the spitting, whether the artist
or the god puts the spirit in the stone, so that what would otherwise be a
"curt and deformed" mannikin becomes as unfathomable and spirited as
starlight and beastsheen. Rilke's Eranna sings to Sappho, the singer: "O
you . . . hurler! / Like a spear among other things / I lay among my kin.
Your music / launched me far. I don't know *where* I am." The animating
and destabilizing of object in event is the very motion of poetry. Sub-
versive of grammatical analysis, it finds its life in the object qua subject,
through poetic passage.

Loss of definition (in from outside, self from other), the sense of over-
thrown outline, of Being full of what exceeds it—these effects permeate
the poem "Eastern Aubade."

> Is this bed we're on not like a sea coast,
> just a strip of coast on which we're stranded?
> Nothing is certain except your high breasts,
> which mounted dizzily beyond my feeling.
>
> For this night, in which so much cried out,
> in which beasts call and tear at one another,
> does its strangeness not dismay us? And yet:
> what's slowly starting up outside (they call it day)—
> do we understand it any better?
>
> We would have to lie as deeply intertwined
> as flower petals around the stamen:
> for the uncontained is everywhere,
> and it gathers force and plunges toward us.
>
> But while we're pressed against each other,
> to keep from seeing how it closes in,
> it may flare out of you, out of me:
> for our souls live on treason.

Interesting to compare this poem with love poems of English literature, say Matthew Arnold's "Dover Beach," in which lover uses lover as
a reinforcement in the battle to exclude the world, for comfort or forgetting. Rilke cannot settle for this consolation, this blind equation (you and
I are one us) and opposition (us against them). Just when the lovers most
hope to use each other as protection from the overwhelming that is *without* them, that which is *within* them bursts forth. It is maybe one of the
scariest evocations of orgasm in literature: the strangeness of the night
(its dark, its bestiality) is in them, and then so is day, equally unknown,
equally uncontainable. The uncontainable which seems so exactly equivalent with what's *outside* our outlines, the terrible uncontainable which
seems to be plunging toward us from afar (where we like to place, and
hope to keep, the unknown) suddenly is here inside us. A reader like de
Man astutely remarks the reversals in Rilke's work—the sudden turning
of *out* to *in* and subject to object, before to after, death to life, fiction to
reality, and vice versa.[4] But what de Man calls Rilke's "ambivalence" is,
to my mind, in the nature of poetic language; indeed, art must raise and
ratify this discomfort, this uneasiness, the play of the senses against what
escapes them, or of language around what is unspeakable. Most poets
seem to believe that consciousness is larger than language and many critics
today seem to doubt that it is. For criticism, consciousness is co-extensive
with language (indeed, critical theory might say, to say so is tautological);
whereas the poet's art exists precisely in the refinement of language until
it's able to suggest or trigger uncontainable or inexpressible experiences
of consciousness, depths of presence. Rilke's art, like Emily Dickinson's,
lies in making the constructions that best embody the paradox, or are
most impressed, rhetorically, with the dilemma, and most inexhaustibly
insist on the limits of reference. Such poems set up structures which
operate like perpetual motion machines, enacting poised antinomies—
opposites equally charged, abiding no exclusive resolution, and operating to create fields of force. The polarities or terminals, in other words,
do not annihilate each other's meanings; and we live in the charged field
between them, so instead of the vertigo of neither we can have the elec-
tricity of both. That is not, as some theorists would have it, the failure of
language, but its power.

*

In "The Marble-Wagon" Rilke writes: ". . . the never-moved is changing . . . And keeps on / drawing near and makes everything stop dead."
Here the exchange (the interpenetration) of opposites is momentous: the

never-moved is moving, and the daily commerces stop dead before it. These are almost already the terms of life as individuals experience it, if the never-moved is death, and the everything is the life we never thought would stop. In the "never-moved" we have the figure of monumental origin itself, the very grounds of being, the rock from which heroic figures are made—the Unmoved, the Ideal—that ultimate a careless reader might mistake for Rilke's privileged metaphysical notion. But it is a figure that, approaching the human scale and life, threatens it.

The Marble-Wagon

Parcelled out on seven drawing horses,
the never-moved is changing into paces;
for what dwells proudly in the marble's core
of age, resistance, and totality

comes forth among men. And look,
we recognize it, beneath whatever name:
just as the hero's sudden interruption
first makes clear to us the drama's thrust:

so it's coming through the day's congested
course, coming in full pomp and retinue,
as though a mighty conqueror were slowly

drawing near at last; and slowly before him
captives, heavy with his weight. And keeps on
drawing near and makes everything stop dead.

I think this poem reveals Rilke's fierce (almost Nietzschean) resistance to comforting narratives of theology, or a metaphysical priority. In this poem, the never-moved (surely that mountain exists only in the mind!) is being dragged around, some kind of modern god, the fallen kind, like Lenin's statue (footloose suddenly, its famously pointing finger now aimless). A not inconsiderable irony of the revolutions in Russia and eastern Europe at the end of the twentieth century had to do with the replacement of the rocks of monumental ideology and power by the rock that is the people's music (a pattern of uncertain footings is the dance of democracy); and one feature of that depedestalization is the accession of youth culture politics and commerce's dehistoricization: the wall of immovability suddenly a commercial collection of chips, both eminently movable and marketable.

In the Rilke poem, the never-moved is not yet sculpted into any idol's shape. It is the source and not the end of monuments. This marble provides material from which we make our statues of heroes, and the hero's "thrust" is to interrupt the drama of the daily. The marble has the weight of priority itself; but its burden of totality is "parcelled out," to go among people. The people, in its presence, stop dead. Men may yearn to believe in, but cannot live by, the monolithic ground or Unmoved Mover. They can't stand up to the Ideal.

The German *Abgrund* (the abyss) is the absence of ground: it is toward the abyss that everything falls. The grounds of the ideal we imagine to be immaterial, the stuff of spirit; but Rilke makes that vacancy take on the greatest weight. Rilke knows the *burden* of God's word (one need only take a look at the poem "A Prophet" to see the stresses conferred by the sacred on the mortal). Embodied, the ideal must be made of the hardest stuff, marble, something to outlast time (so the immortal gets figured, paradoxically, in the densest material).

Marble's story of origins has the same power for us as does the figure of the hero himself, whose shape will be made of marble's matter. The hero is always a synechdoche, meant to convey in his person the Whole (though the human figure is partial). In "A Prophet," as we'll see, God's human spokesman, like Cassandra, bears the gift as a curse, vomiting God's truth like chunks of volcanic rock, with a splitting headache made literal, as the human forehead tries to contain the thought of God. Here, in the thought of God, the objective and subjective genitive, interpenetrating, become unbearable.

In "The Marble-Wagon" the drama is played on the stage of daily life, *as if* to conquer it. The victims of such burdens, those who have to bear the weight of the unformed stuff from which the heroic is to be carved, those who have to feel the constraints of such constructions, are present to give scale to the atrocity, to keep the Ideal ironized. The closer the enormity gets, the deader human commerces and life become. The tyranny of history's impositions of ideals on the hapless individual human figure, flawed and vulnerable, is the bitter source of this poem—no unquestioning reverence for founding forms, Platonic or religious, can be said to inform this vision. The drama's thrust is toward the stopping-dead of life: *that* is what "dwells proudly in the marble's core." For Rilke as for Nietzsche, the Christian church, its rock of the ideal, resembles nothing so much as an enormous gravestone. God will hurt and kill us, if life doesn't do it first. Who can read "A Prophet" and not feel that bitter belief at work?

A Prophet

Stretched wide by gigantic visions,
bright from the fire's glare from that course
of judgements, which never destroy him,—
are his eyes, gazing beneath thick
brows. And already in his inmost self
words are building up again,

not his own (for what would his amount to
and how benignly they'd go to waste)
but other, hard ones: chunks of iron, stones,
which he must melt down like a volcano

in order to throw them out in the outbreak
of his mouth, which curses and curses,
while his forehead, like a dog's forehead,
tries to bear *that*

which the Lord from his own forehead takes:
This God, This God, whom they would all find,
if they'd follow the huge pointing hands
that reveal Him as He is: enraged.

A stunningly brutal (one might say sacrilegious) view—based on God's wrath as inscribed in Old Testament accounts—but cruelly foreshortened, to expose its distorting pressure on the human figure. This God has volcanic force, and makes the man a vomiter, a dog, a spewer of hardness and heat, as if from the center of the earth (where Dante places hell). For man to bear THAT, to bear the inconceivable (which God is, if we take Christianity literally), he must be racked. Its power and its revelations come not from outside, but from his "inmost self," just as destructive lava erupts from the inmost earth. Who can say which is the ground of which? Does the lava make the earth, or the earth the lava? Does the God inside make the man, or the man make the God inside? If this is spirituality, it will not turn away from the brutal lights of the material world. It recalls Nietzsche's saying, of the universe, "How could we reproach or praise (it)? Let us beware of attributing to it heartlessness and unreason or their opposites: it is neither perfect nor beautiful, nor noble, nor does it wish to become any of these things. It does not strive to imitate man. None of our aesthetic or moral judgments apply to it."[5]

The voice of ordinary authority can handle the comprehensible, the graspable, the seizable; but with Rilke the soul does not seize God, the soul is seized into God. What is inmost and what is outermost are equally incomprehensible, and our lives are framed between.

The Rose Window

In there: the lazy pacing of their paws
creates a stillness that's almost dizzying;
and the way then suddenly one of the cats
takes the gaze that keeps straying from it

overpoweringly into its own great eye,—
and that gaze, as if seized by a whirlpool's
circle, stays afloat for a little while
and then sinks and knows itself no longer,

> when this eye, which only seems to rest
> opens and slams shut with a roar
> and tears it all the way inside the blood—:
>
> in the same way long ago the cathedrals'
> great rose windows would seize a heart
> from the darkness and tear it into God.

Here the gaze that wants to stray is ours, the onlooker's, and the eye that captures it is at once the eye of an animal and the eye of God. Rilke once again (as in "Archaic Torso of Apollo") frames the missing human element between stone and star, between fire and fur. The statue's sensual surface in "Archaic Torso," remember, was compared to everything but the human skin it represents. (Rilke surrounds his absent object the way Capa does—he captures its traces and effects on bystanders, on onlookers, on attendant human being.) In his object (that object so likely to slip into subject, as the statue does, and as the rose window will) we lose ourselves, in an annihilation intimately related to a death; that is why he invokes the wild animal, the dangerous whirlpool. And all of these figures are full of paradox—spirit and flesh, still and dizzying, seeing and seen—the spectator at the same moment seen, and the one reaching out at the same moment seized. All our daily inclination to be idle tourists, to be comfortable believers, our inclination to tame art or spirit or the unspeakable by *comprehending* it, turns on us. For the uncontainable is everywhere, as Rilke loves to tell us; it is even in ourselves.

That's why the poem "The Rose Interior" moves from expansion's question ("Where for this Inside is there / an Outside?") to the poem's final contract (not contraction) of paradox ("until all of summer becomes / a room, a room within a dream"). We mean to keep the dream in its place, in the safety of a stored construct, the comfortable narrative we like to tell ourselves about our lives—it is, we console ourselves, all in our mind, in our sleep, in our night, in our room, in our house. But the dream has us, and not the other way around. The scales are reversed, the thing in us is larger than ourselves. To be seized is to be rapt. Its noun is rapture. We think we have experience in hand, in mind; but then everything we made secure is nothing, and nothing seizes us. This otherness is in us as the hollows are in the hands of the beggars.

It is for this discovery (the discovery that the true focus of the moment of art is not on an object but on a subject, that the missing center is not in the title but in the reader) that one loves the photographs of Robert Capa so much. One of his most terrible and eloquent photos is of a group of soldiers crossing a minefield. The field is ordinary, the shot is one of a thousand he must have taken and discarded in his life as a photographer on front lines everywhere. But this one is informed by what came after it. It was the last he ever took, and was shot a few hundred feet from the ground which would explode, killing him. That knowledge, coming from the future back into the photograph, informs it terribly for the viewer who knows Capa never saw it printed. As we live, as artists and sensitive readers of art, we cast our object ahead of us, as if it were seizable by will; but we must be seized, ourselves, must be inscribed as we inscribe. There is some at-onceness which is presence—partaking of past and future and something unlocatable, in time—at work in the work that moves us most. In it we recognize the inseparable claims of inward and outward, sayable and unsayable, seeable and unseen.

*

My greatest pleasure in studying the "Tour de France" diptych occurred on the edge of the unseen. It occurred in a glimpse that changed all the other moments for me and gave me the jolt of a revealed ideal, glimpse of the stilled thing, absence materialized. Within the rush of my seeing, with its busy intentions and connections, the noise of the before-and-after, breeze in newspapers, faces looking forward and then looking after, the speed with which presence has gone rushing by—beyond all that there is, still, a sign of the presence that stays. In anticipation, you can't see it, though the anticipators have it in mind. Only after the actual bypassing of the bicyclists, only after the brush with the whoosh of the experienced, only, in other words, after THEY see them, can we see *it*: it was hidden by the postures of looking forward, and revealed by the turn to look after. These witnesses have their backs to the only form of the occasioning object we as readers could see: the stilled apparatus all this reference was about ("art is about something," says Allen Grossman, "the way a cat's about the house"): image of pure potential, sign seized out of time. It was there all along, the mechanism of the missing subject/object, figure for the art itself, there all along in the photo's window. It is a kind of present for us; over against the occasion as passage, it does not pass. After we have registered the brimming breezes of the passage (subject always moving out of object), we see again, by virtue of still photography's medium, the sign of the mind's abiding occasion: a time that stays as idea, out of the stream of motions in time. Convinced we'd got the point (the object missed, but adumbrated in surroundings), were we, after all, the ones who failed to see?

One last look at a Rilkean passage, before we close.

Encounter in the Chestnut Avenue

He felt the entrance's green darkness
wrapped coolly around him like a silken cloak
that he was still accepting and arranging:
when at the opposite transparent end, far off,

through green sunlight, as through green windowpanes,
whitely a solitary shape
flared up, long remaining distant
and then finally, the downdriving light
boiling over it at every step,
bearing on itself a bright pulsation,
which in the blond ran shyly to the back.
But suddenly the shade was deep,
and nearby eyes lay gazing

from a clear new unselfconscious face,
which, as in a portrait, lived intensely
in the instant things split off again:
first there forever, and then not at all.

In the poem, as in the Capa diptych, the encounter is phenomenally exact, yet turns about an absence: this image of another figure entering the passage (in both pieces, the passage is of space as well as time) in which an orienting consciousness has paused, is touched with the *Blendung* which in German means at once dazzling vision and blinding vision. The figure of the Other has from afar something of the aspect of a ghost: it enters the passage from the far end, after all, and not the entrance, and boils, as sunlit figures seem to do when viewed from shady tunnels, with the light that seems to constitute its being and annihilate its features. As our vantage stays with the first and forward-going figure, this Other seems to move in time, from the future toward the present, until it approaches so close it too enters the shade of proximity: the deepest shade is nearest the self, and the new face, suddenly seen in detail, passes virtually into the self's own unseeability. (Remember how invisible the very near can be; at its limits it is as unseen as the very far-off is: we cannot see our own eyes). The moment when the object turns to subject—when the other and the self become indistinguishable, that moment which the sorting logics of an analytical language cannot register, when the lyrical recourse is paradox, that moment ("as in a portrait," Rilke tells us, or, we might add, in the held present of a photograph), that time "lived intensely in the instant," an instant in which "things split off." It is a moment of birth, when inner is borne into outer, outer into inner; for self and other are born together, both at once, when as infant organisms we first distinguish ourselves. This moment has its own dark flash of insight, as if two times became simultaneous (the future entered the past), two became beings-at-once, as if (indeed) we could imagine birth at both extremes of existence's passage—all these temporal effects flash through this moment of encounter. The other enters and departs from the self, and the usual sense of life's passage (from nothing to something) is reversed: the other, like the self, is "first there forever, and then not at all." Something timeless becomes nothing ever.

Look back at the "passage" Capa provides us, framing the stream of the bicyclists' going-by, to show us how things looked before and after them. What of this occasion DON'T we see? The instrument of motion? The vehicle itself (which is, in some form, in art always "behind" performance)? It was present here all along—the spectators lining the street turn FROM its sign because they are drawn into its motion.

For what we didn't see isn't what is *outside* the frame of vision: most viewers are sophisticated enough to read the other signs, and focus on the missingness. We are even sophisticated enough to muse that there are two kinds of missing made the point here—the missing before something's been seen, and the missing after: the bicyclists were at first anticipated, *un*appeared; and then the bicyclists were remembered, *dis*appeared. But the missing we do ourselves, when something's right before our eyes, that's the missing we miss (as viewers, not only as thinkers). If we watch the watchers closely, then their turning reveals something behind it all, resisting disappearance even now. Look into the lens of the window behind them: it is still *there*. It is *still* there. The storefront contains the stilled image of the missing (it's the store of the idea, not the action; and the idea is persistent). Look again, and you'll see! It delivers a gift, a hidden twist toward us, from the missing subject and the missing artist: its handlebars and gearshifts visible, the store is a bicycle store!

Tour de France, Pleyben, Brittany, July 1939. Photo by Robert Capa. Permission granted by Magnum Photos, Inc.

The Still Pool Forgets

A Reminding from the Yoruba

The Yoruba people of western Africa, one of the largest ethnic popu-
lations south of the Sahara, constitute a powerful urban culture.
Yoruba cities fostered rich economic, administrative, and religious systems, and it was precisely this society the western slave trade plundered
for human wealth: nearly all slaves brought to the Americas came from
west Africa, and of these, Yoruba slaves and their descendants became a
most significant influence in the cultures of Cuba, Brazil, and other parts
of the Americas, including the United States.

What these Africans brought with them was a deep and practical regard for the arts. In Yoruba cities, sophisticated systems of exchange
and distribution had made markets for weaving, dyeing, iron-working,
brass-casting, woodcarving, beadwork, leatherwork, and pottery; arts
networks grew wide and interdependent. Even Yoruba hunters were said
to praise the gifts of those who carve wood or compose song; proficiency
in these arts was valued as highly as bravery and warrior skills. Among the
social features of Yoruba life were powerful polygamous family systems,
and the pre-eminence of older women as magicians and spell-binders.
Professional distinction was accorded singers or poets, who were responsible for perpetuating and embellishing the stories of gods and notable

mortals, figures such as Shango (God of Thunder), Ogun (God of Iron), and Eshu (God of Fate). In New Orleans and New York today you can find shops in which are sold images of Ogun, god of hunters, warriors, professional circumcisers, all who make use of his metal. From the totemic figure dangle tiny knives and hoes and hammers and machinery-parts; in him many ages meet.

Both gods and men can be appeased. Among the functions of the professional poets is the making of honorific names. Unlike naming in patronymic cultures, Yoruba naming occurs not only before and at birth, but after. There is the name that comes from circumstances of the birth (the-one-with-the-cord-around-his-neck, let us say); there is the name recording the parents' (sometimes unsentimental) sentiments about the event (the-straw-that-broke-the-camel's-back). And there is the third kind of name: *oriki*. These names are a form of pet-naming, praise-naming, poetic name; and though praise names may be assigned at birth, they are earned all through life. A very notable figure may garner many such names, and very great trees, cities, or gods are paid tribute by professional oriki-makers. Ulli Beier (to whose indispensable work I owe my acquaintance with Yoruba poetry) gives, by way of example of oriki, the name these poets gave to the first European explorers in Africa: "a pair of shorts that can worry a large embroidered gown."[6] It is an immediately funny and yet painful reminder of colonial history, coded into a practically succinct, semiotic garb.

I mean to celebrate the practical premises of this work. To the ear and mind of someone brought up on English and American poetry, it seems refreshingly direct—full of humor, wit, and intricate exemplification. Abstraction operates to bespeak, not to outspeak, physical experience. In poems of considerable structural complexity, poems that operate as pulsing signs for human understanding, this ground of Yoruba metaphysics is moving. Yoruba singers and drummers set up powerful long-distance communications (CNN watch out): songs can actually change fates (some 600 gods, after all, are listening; and they can be tickled, pleased, seduced). All the Yoruba gods but one (the unapproachable Olodumare) are variable, mischievous, and yet amusable; and all can kill—there is a god, for example, of smallpox. All are also respected and honored, and there results a peculiar mix of affection and insult that resembles nothing so much as familial relations. Not unlike human beings in their gifts and foibles, Yoruba gods are responsible for love and trouble both. The Yoruba value generosity as wealth, and even their religion seems touched with this liberality. The poems to the gods can't get too predictable or pious, because the gods themselves don't: among the originary stories of Yoruba mythology, for example, the occasional tendency of the gods, like human beings, to drink too much and then make compositional mistakes explains how white people came to be.

Riddles and songs collected from very young Yoruba children suggest how free from prurience are subjects America tends to hold taboo. Beier cites the song told him by a six-year-old girl, used by little girls to drive boys away from their play:

> Penis penis plays by himself
> Vagina vagina plays by herself.
> We shall not play with somebody
> Who has sixteen testicles.

Two children's riddles for which the answer is "vagina" are: "a small bearded god, whom we must kneel to worship," and "a little bush becomes a court case." From infancy to old age, the Yoruba sensibility is tickled with the carnal comedies.

*

I'm not a scholar of Yoruba language or culture. I can't judge the fidelity of the translations used here (all taken from Ulli Beier's remarkable collection of Yoruba poems, divinations, chants and proverbs), nor offer social or political elaboration on the context. I refer interested readers to Beier's work, and in particular to his descriptions of the pitches and rhythms of "talking" drums. My intention is simply to appreciate a few of the poetic texts Beier has given us, taking the texts as artifacts provocative in (and to) English. What these pieces did to me was strike at the heart of my sense of the poetic; they worked like an antidote to overdose. (I mean the overdose of polite nostalgias and predictable discretions in contemporary American poetry.) These brief Yoruba pieces make an extraordinary contrast to our poetry-magazine-multitudes because of their directness, their practical relation to the material world, their freedom from self-absorbed nostalgia or perennial regret. In them, one senses the force of an efficacious act, and not an art in the process of its own elegizing. They proceed by a kind of structural logic and natural analogy that seems based on human beings being treated as only one form of being among others; there's plenty to learn from plants and animals, as well as from gods, who are (in the Yoruba cosmology) no more fickle than weather (and no less). Poetry itself takes on the patterns of such creaturehood; it mimics, honors, and affects nature. For the Yoruba, far more fundamentally than for contemporary Americans, poetry has daily force as a human form of nature.

*

Death

I cannot carry it,
I cannot carry it.
If I could carry it,
I would carry it.
When the elephant dies in the bush
something is carried into the house.
When the buffalo dies in the forest,
something is carried into the house.
But when the mouse dies in the house
something is thrown into the bush.

Note here first of all, in the best sense, the beating-around-the-bush. The bush is a literal location, and the poem doesn't metaphorize away a difficult question. It is stunning, immediately, for the directness of its address to the sorrow at hand. Apart from the natural analogical relation that arises between title and body of poem, there is in the poem no direct statement that the repeated "it" is the burden of death itself. Indeed, the virtue of the poem lies entirely in its refusal to abstract its object: the physical weight of the death, and not its philosophical constitution, seems at issue, and the repetition "I cannot carry" builds up great power, as if in plain linguistic illustration of a Dickinsonian numbness-in-the-face-of-death. In concentrating less on the idea than on the body of death, this poem distinguishes itself clearly from most American elegies or meditations on the subject: there is a kind of death math here, as if physically to "grasp" or "bear" its dimensions.

The poetic move from animal to human—inevitable in hundreds of American road-kill poems—is left, blessedly, implicit in this Yoruba death-chant; and a kind of humor (almost unthinkable in this connection in America, where the unbearability of death is itself unmentionable) obtains in the sudden disposability of the domestic corpse, the brief heft and trajectory of mouse.

The trail of analogies is also a trail of changes, and the play of parallels enacts a pattern of repetition and variation that is complex in implication. The animals become progressively lighter, but also progressively closer to home. Not only how big they are but how near us they live becomes important. What death means to us, in ranges unenclosed, is what we can carry off: from the death of the elephant and buffalo much can be made, much can be redeemed. But from the deaths closest to us, what salvage? Deaths inside the human house are removed into the outer world; deaths in the outer are (at least in part) brought in.

Paradoxically enough, the most portable deaths are of the biggest, farthest animals. The verb "carried" is insistent, occurring in six of the poem's ten lines; and in the last line of the poem suddenly it is replaced by "thrown"—this accounts for at least part of the shock of levity at the end. Of these large and far-off deaths, something (quantities of something, tusk or meat) can be taken in. (We live on—live off—the deaths of things outside; we are their grave.) But of the deaths "in the house" something is thrown out. We don't eat the mouse, or use the hide of the dead domestic cat; deaths in the psychological interior have to be pushed out of mind, so we can live. The poem suggests how big a little thing can be, close-up (the closest deaths are the least bearable, is a fair paraphrase in English). The line thus drawn between the domestic (even the domestic "wild" animal like the mouse) and the outside world (even its most amicable animals) is a clear and inviolable line, physical, psychological, and spiritual.

The four *it*s and the three *something*s seem brilliantly, intently non-specific. They are not vague, as so many somethings are in contemporary poetry (wanting to evoke the bodiless unnameable, wanting, in short, to get a big feeling out of a small abdication). Here the somethings are bodily parts, more or less simply. But a principle, an equation, even, is being worked out, and it is the pattern of carryings, not the content or mystification of them, that is most important to the Yoruba poem. Indeed these words insist on looking not at private but at a sum of public gestures, and rather than evading the difficulty of naming, slipping from the letter toward the spirit, they do an exacter, weirder work: a kind of framing, very physical. In contemporary American poetry, "something" crops up as poetic phrasing around powerful mysteries: something told me she was dead; something moved in the shadows; there was something red about the night, etc. It partakes of our mistake about the great mysteries, assuming that they inhere in the spirit and not in the letter of things. In short, in our poetry, a "something" is seldom so meant: it is more like a nothing, its drift is atmospheric, its vicinity the failed ideal. One feels American poets have deeply lost their faith in the physical power of words. Culturally that power seems most directly to obtain in the arenas of advertising and public relations, the very arenas from which most American poets are by nature and by economic association most deeply alienated—and the realm popularly accorded poetry, that of sentiment, is represented in America by the million-fold small-surprise industry of the greeting card. We don't, as a rule, make even our own prayers, or value freshness or invention in them. If we believe in God, we don't believe in a God that would change his mind. The much mentioned "personality" of American life—your "personal" banker, your "personal" God—seems deeply, perhaps pathologically, impersonal. And our prudishness with regard to sex—its unmentionability intimate with the industry of pornography, making much of private parts and making of property the most sacred place—resembles nothing so much as our way of dealing with death. A very fundamental loneliness comes of the displacements of sex and death into dark back rooms, into solitudes, into chambers where tissues and towels are dispensed for secret blottings out, and from which the yearner or mourner returns to sunlit—loveless, deathless—streets, wiped clean of carnal attachment and animal relation.

Compare that world, its models of animal life, and the world of the poem that follows:

Quarrel

Nobody will quarrel with the woodcock,
because of his blue coat.
Nobody will quarrel with the parrot
because of his red tail.
You old people of this world,
don't be my enemies.
Would you kill a dog because he barks?
Would you kill a ram because he butts?
Would you kill the goat because he fucks his mother?
Forgive me, don't fight,
and let me taste the world
like the fly that interprets the wine . . .

One loves this song's sense of necessary conviviality in the grips of sex and death. Its funniness and feel of fable arise from patterns of analogy, and there are, in the translation, wonderful ambiguities that arise because we don't know exactly where to attach the *becauses*. (Beier gives us one of each—placing a comma before the first and not the second.) Is the red tail the sign that warns off quarrel, or is the red tail (the blue coat) the *content* of the quarrel? In the latter case, the "taster of the world" (the lover of barking and butting and fucking) argues that his pleasures are his very fur and feather, his very nature and stripe; no one can quarrel with what is so much a matter of born identity. In either case, the coat and tail are flashed as signs: they serve as the poet's defense against those "old people."

The oldsters have their own say about sartorial flourish. "A young man can have a robe like an elder's, but he can't have rags like an elder's," so the elders tell us. Notice what dignities accrue to the old—not the fancy clothes, or big pension, or store-bought Winnebago; any money can buy those. But the way we age, the way we wear and weather, those are ours alone. You can't get store-bought rags. They take years to perfect (that is, to undo). It is a wisdom that turns the meaning of wealth inside-out, and knows how *nouveau* material senses of *riche* can be.

Patterns of repetition and variation account for much of the momentum and charge of "Quarrel"; the trail that leads to the shock of "fucks his mother" has proceeded by analogue, sidewindingly innocent (barks worsens into butts, but remains a feature of animal nature; butts worsens into fucks, and suddenly fucks appropriates an object from the realm of the human taboo). Imagine the encounter between moral niceties of missionary, and this lively forthrightness. To my mind, it is reminiscent of the transcripts we do have of encounters between English officer/lawyers and the native Americans they were trying to convince to sign real estate contracts that would, ultimately, keep the tribes from hunting— even though the tribes were promised they'd retain such rights. At the end of the negotiations, in which one witnesses the arts of legal interest at work—arts of representation and persuasion that would later flower into advertising's soul and industry on those same American valleys and plains—and during whose proceedings one sees clearly the respect the native American elders pay their visitors before agreeing to what they clearly understand would mean sharing the land—at the very end of all of these negotiations, a sign appears more telling than the legal signatures. The tribal elder remarks, as he makes his assenting mark on the documents, that the parties must concur on equal footing, being men who share the sense of a single God, men equal under the same God. Whereupon the English officer in attendance replies, in effect: "Very good. We'll send in missionaries to educate you." It is a moment of pure hubris on the part of the English, a moment in which one can't help wincing at their self-absorption, their indelicacy.

Though one can imagine the ways a merely moralizing reader might dismiss the barks-butts-fucks propositions as crude, and never detect the poem's fundamental subtlety and humanity, the last few lines of this Yoruba poem "Quarrel" are as acute, as refined and refining, as any I know. It's a young man's poem to the old, remember, and the address that was begun in lines 5 and 6, with "you old people of this world / don't be my enemies," now reaches its culmination in "Forgive me, don't fight, / and let me taste the world." This young man, though flashing his fighting form, is eschewing battle, and asking the elders' blessing on those other energies of youth (barking, butting, fucking, in full fettle, finest feather—asking a blessing, that is, not on death-dealing but life-loving acts, acts of argument and sport and love). The last two lines ("and let me taste the world / like the fly that interprets the wine") enact a powerful shift of scale. Like the trail in "Death" that led from tragedy of elephant to comedy of mouse, this poem's thrust includes a sudden turn: after waving red flags, brandishing blues, and generally making much young-male bravado, it comes down to a refinement all the more endearing for taking place on a fly's lip: the molecule of wine the sipper savors (and, in savoring, considers) is, though tiny, yet significant. And the word "interprets" is a gorgeous translatorial move; it takes on added elegance for referring to a feature of the poetic (and readerly) caretaking going on even as we read. The poem, like the world, keeps being remade, fresh and actual, in the senses of its interpreters.

The poem's claims on us are finally funnily disarming, for the speaker who had preened and charged and strutted through the poem turns both as refined as a wine-taster and as humble as a Musca Domestica. It is the wine of the *world* that is celebrated finally, and that emphasis establishes the true spirit of the poem. Consider the disinclination of so many contemporary American poems either to comedies of bravado or to the savor of a joyous carnality, and you realize why Yoruba poems can so much refresh us. To the extent that they are most interested in private emotion and personal nostalgia, our poets have forgotten how to move; and to the extent that they've lost that capacity to transport and to be transported, they've forgotten how to swing beyond the singular, and sing.

*

It is revealing to examine the kind of proverbs the Yoruba people tell. Some Yoruba proverbs have a lot in common with the sayings of European elders. (After all, there is a community of experience in the body of old age, and sometimes elders resemble their counterparts in other societies more than they do the young ones in their own.) It might as well be Yiddish, the Yoruba saying "He who shits on the way will find flies on the way back." But there are characteristic Yoruba proverbs that seem, on the other hand, refreshingly unEuropean in their moral motions: "A person fetching water from a pool says he saw somebody wearing a mask. What will he say who fetches water from a stream?" The art of Yoruba masquerade has its own formulaic tradition, but the universal logic of this riddle already richly suggests the reflective comparison between still and running water, and asks the agile mind to consider, in the manner of the Zen koan, the reflection to be had when one draws one's image not from holdings, but from flowing and change.

Or consider this: "The thinking of a wolf is enough to kill a sheep." It is one of those translations one loves the more for its double reading, for both the subjective genitive (the wolf's thought) and the objective genitive (the sheep's thought about the wolf) work to make the proverb's points: in the former case, the wolf's power goes beyond tooth and claw, and in the latter case, the point is about the victim's complicity in his own demise: for fear can cause its own heart attack. In either case, the proverb reminds us that the mind can be the sharpest weapon, whether you use it to attack another or to attack yourself.

The one I love best, I guess, because it has the signature Yoruba twists in it, from raucous outburst to wry insight, is this: "The worm is dancing, but that is only how he walks." Yoruba poems as a genre seem forthright, going straight to the dance of the matter; skeptical about human nature, not so full of themselves they fool themselves.

Tricks

The star is trying to outshine the moon,
the frog is preparing a trick to get wings,
the one who wears a cotton dress pretends to wear velvet,
the one who is wearing velvet pretends to be a king.
We all try to do
what God never intends us to do.
Watch out: "We shall catch and kill"
is what we cry when we go to the battlefield.
We tend to forget that we shall meet another man there
uttering the same cry . . .

It is this capacity to see things from the other perspective suddenly that puts the best kind of nation in imagination; it is an integrating capacity one might call love, if love in English didn't seem first and foremost narrowly self-interested. Yoruba children's songs are full of this dance of ironies and empathies, right from the beginning. Keep in mind that what the cow is to the English, the yam is to the Yoruba, and lend an ear to the happy yammer (no cower) who made this children's song:

Yam

Yam, yam, yam,
You are of pure white.
You have a gown of meat,
You have a cap of vegetables,
You have trousers of fish.
Yam, oh yam, oh yam.

Or, in the same connection, but in another poem, consider the fledging generosity, forgiveness and rueful natural knowledge involved in the following children's song about the hapless baby, Lagbada:

Housetraining

Lagbada shits in the house
We do not blame him
Lagbada pisses in the house
We do not blame him.
But the flies will give him away.
The flies will give him away.

Intra- and inter-generational conversations are conducted frequently in Yoruba songs and poems. Here is one that demonstrates many of the poetic idiosyncrasies I've highlit in other poems: it is full of the analogical and parallel structures we've seen elsewhere, yet also full of irrepressible expansiveness, lucid mysteries.

Memory

Whatever I am taught,
let me remember it.
When the big fish comes out of the water
we can see the bottom of the pond.
When the big toad comes out of the water
we can see the bottom of the well.
When the kingfisher dives into the water
his brain becomes clear.
When the cheek of the pregnant antelope was marked
her child was also marked.
If there is one piece of meat left in the pot
it will surely be taken by the spoon.
Everything the landlord does
is known to the swallow.
Everything that is in your brain,
my father,
let it be known to me.

This one's mysteries are lucid in *time*. It is no accident that in the world of the poet who could write such a poem, the god of fate, Ishu, is able to "throw a stone today and kill a bird yesterday." The poem is called "Memory" and like all poems asks its reader to circle from its end back to its beginning: in the father's brain is what the son will need, a kind of future made of past. The markings of the antelope are communicated to her child, in genetic memory; and though people may argue about who gets the last piece of meat in the pot (who lives longest), still the spoon (the carrier) survives them all.

There is subtle play on content and container here: the pond and well contain clarity the way the mind, able to remember, does. In order to remember, you take, paradoxically, something *out*—the big fish or the big toad—its motion and dimension can only muddy the water. The toad is amphibian, it will come and go, whereas the fish will probably come out only once. But either way the big animal has to be gotten out (or has to, himself, get out) before the medium of memory can become calm enough to be clear.

When the third variation in the repetitive series comes ("when the kingfisher dives into the water / his brain becomes clear"), the change wrought against the parallels and repetition is, first and foremost, directional: an animal *enters* instead of *leaving* the water, adding a body in order to subtract one, and can then, himself, take on the attribute of clarity. In a sense, the water's transparency enters *him*. This is the magic of sympathy. Symmetrically, the kingfisher can keep reentering to *clear* what the toad keeps reentering to *muddy*; and the kingfisher's brain becomes a predatory single-mindedness, its aim clear (just as the poet hopes in the medium of the poem to narrow and clarify his own object, and thus turn it into subject). The bird, in taking on the attributes of the fish it seeks, becomes not only what it enters (the medium of the water, which continues to seem the mind's medium or memory), but also becomes what *enters it*. The flyer swims *like* the fish it will eat, but also *toward* the fish it will eat, and, taking it out, takes it in.

Remembering the title, we have to assume that the spatial relations between mind and memory are more complex than we might usually think: mind doesn't only contain memories; that is, memories don't only swim in the mind. Memory is itself the medium in which the mind swims. In this dimensional inside-outness, the Yoruba manage to catch the almost uncorralable qualities a sophisticated European philosophical tradition has such trouble finding words for: the slippage involved in speaking about language in language, or having mind in mind. Finally it is not the landlord who knows most about the house; his superior is the house-swallow, who can come and go and is above landlordian notice. (The tenants will not escape the landlord so easily, and will suffer the levies and taxes of private property; but the bird is elevated, and flies in and out of the head of the house.) As if by sympathetic suggestion, after this series of insights into the insides (and overlords) of things, the poet prays to know what his father knows. The wish is quietly spoken at last, but means to incorporate the past in order to bear the future.

There is a Yoruba recitation for mourning. It goes like this:

He is lost to us through death
is a cry full of pain; I will walk,
talking to myself in a low voice.

It is not just the quietness of this mourning that so endears us to it. It is
not just the wisdom that knows not to wail too loud. It is the subtlety
of turns of mind in the poem. The pause after the first line's conventional opening, "He is lost to us through death," turns the whole cry into
a cry examined as an act of language—for the second line removes the
mourner from the cry and effectively puts quotes about the first line, as
if it could be examined from outside the pain. This is Donne's "for saying so," the second turn in The Triple Fool's self-admonition: "I am two
fools, I know, for loving and for saying so." Like Donne, the Yoruba wise
man knows "the best fool" is as wise as we get. As soon as the Yoruba
speaker identifies "He is lost to us through death" as a cry full of pain, he
immediately (mid-line) tries to dispense with that cry: if this is crying, he
seems to decide, I'm walking.

But just when the poem seems, in line 2, to have turned away from
utterance (which in commemorating, perpetuates pain) and toward motion (as if *e*motion could be outwalked), the third line returns to the
voice. Like Donne, he'll soften the pain by lowering the decibel, rather
than raising it; he continues the song, but to himself (which is after all
where death still lives). In the face of death, he turns to himself: the song
switches from a loud-crying-toward-others to a low-reflexive-talking.

It is a model of the very nature of elegy: the person one yearns to talk
to cannot hear, no loudness of cry or fastness of running can bring the
mourner near enough to the mournee. If he talks to himself, it is because
he knows in time he is headed where the dead one went; by talking to
himself he is talking to the one who is gone, the future being a remembered, or a carried-forward, past. The subject of the poem "Death," with
which we began this celebration of Yoruba poems ("When the elephant
dies in the bush . . ."), is here addressed vis à vis the human loss, which
is to say vis à vis the self. Where before one bore the elephant, now one
bears the weight of death in (and as) one's own body.

That self being talked to is a self containing much more than the
conventional contemporary American poetic self which, when it talks
to itself, is either crazy or self-centered, talking to number one, yours
truly, the only apple of its eye. But the math of self for Yoruba poets
is both more and less than the number one—it is full of the memory
the mind sought out from its mothers and fathers, and full of the future

sympathetically invoked; it is full of the studied ways of animals and the brushes with propitiated gods, as causal as casual, fatal as funny. It's full of singing out, and singing in, and full of a wry sense that all of our ins-and-outs (contents in containers, meanings in meaners, words in words) may be so much misdirection. One of the oracular Yoruba poets says (in Wordsworthian wisdom, if not brevity): "If a parent has begotten a child, however long it might take, the child may yet beget the parent." Such constructions of self permit it to shift in and out of the media in which it operates (distinctions of time and number, for example, which range for us somewhere between none and three) and so encourage fluidities of mental category. The past and present and future, no matter how firmly and exclusively erected in the structures of a grammar, remind us that they were, after all, filled from changing streams.

The proud European philosophical and literary tradition has come to a point of (maybe fatal) suffering from its capture in its own reflexive men-tal mechanisms, tending to close in about itself in its quest for a legal self, the privatest extension of the principle of property. For such a sensibility, this Yoruba self, this open border (self so full, finally, of otherness) feels salutary, fresh, releasing. There is a proverb I think catches something of the stillness and the motion of the two cultures, and I'll close with it. It is a Yoruba saying that, though mysterious, seems full of love for, and vulnerability to, change; it reminds us of the vanity of the self-made, and the rich refreshments of the moving current. It has the force of a warning about self-circumscription and about the risks of stagnation there. The Yoruba elders put it this way, "The proud pond stands aloof from the river, forgetting."

In that deceptively modest last word lies the gist of the indictment, the point of the *aperçu*. Its wisdom deflates our own readiness to iden-tify with the proud, and makes us remember what the *idée fixe* is full of: trapped fluency from an *idée courante*. I leave you with the words of this Yoruba proverb about the proud pond, knowing I can't be the only one who smells self-absorption in the American pool, and confident the wise will get the drift.

A Stranger's Way of Looking

I

It's one thing to be alone, and quite another to be deserted. I've always considered any opportunity to spend a stretch of time on islands to be precious, but the difference between solitude and loneliness is sometimes mistaken for the difference between work and love. When G. K. Chesterton was asked what book he'd pick for life on a deserted island, he responded: *"Thomas' Guide to Practical Shipbuilding."* [7]

*

According to Heraclitus, a man is most remote from what he's most continuously in contact with. (This *what* is a woman, my husband remarked.) The artist in particular has always been someone who had to get away in order to understand what he was part of. One must leave town, says Nietzsche, to see how high its towers are. (Remember Wordsworth's rowboat, in *The Prelude*: it had to carry him away a distance before he saw the dimensions of the crag he'd been anchored under.)

But Nietzsche's Zarathustra grows lonely, and contemplates returning from self-imposed exile into the human community. (It is ourselves we humans are farthest away from, Nietzsche will write elsewhere.) And it is apparent that, while the seer may be solitary, the sayer requires an audience. This double impulse, both to and from others, drives—and divides—writing as it does writers. Not only do we have the feeling that every man is an island. But also, since Heidegger, an extra loneliness arises: even when we find conversant company, we come to entertain a modern suspicion: that language is the only one doing the talking.

*

> I think also finally
> Of the silk-noise, solitary, subtle
> Of a fire creating a whole room
> By a self-devouring.
> It speaks to itself.
> Or, almost for its own sake,
> It speaks to me.
>
> Paul Valéry [8]

*

"The rest I leave to silence," says the watchman at the outset of Aeschylus's *Agamemnon*. And then he adds, in a translation English audiences might take to be directed at the very presence of audience: "The house itself, could it take voice, might speak aloud and plain. I speak to those who understand, but if they fail, I have forgotten everything." [9]

What paradoxes of time arise here! If the listeners (in that watchman's future) will not understand, then he (the one whose job it is to pass on signs) *has already forgotten* what he knew. This seems an odd forgetting, a *consequence* of something that happens *after* it—a forgetting caused not by the forgetter's incapacity but by an incapacity in potential co-rememberers. It argues, by implication, for an odd kind of memory—a memory contingent on its seconding in others, cognition needing recognition, according needing recording. Such memory is collective memory, contingent on comparison, confirmation, consensuality—something prefixed with a with. The co-knower, the receiver, is needed to keep the signaller's art and meaning from atrophy.

The memory the watchman speaks of, then, is not only *contingent* (on his speaking being heard and understood, a theme which will arise again and again in this play) but also *expedient*. For a shared understanding is a less dangerous one, and some threats make forgetting safer, for the understander who must otherwise stand it all alone . . .

The watchman is speaking about the perennial condition of art (the muses' mother was Mnemosyne, or memory). If we don't participate with the watchman, with the reader and conveyer of signs, he will forget the art of relaying, relating: and he will forget *for all of us*.

*

The watchman opens the play: he is a figure of the playwright; he is our eyes. A freak of time, he sees what has not yet arrived: he forefigures. Indeed this speech at *Agamemnon*'s outset is the speech that foresees the play's closing, in which the miscreants retreat into a literally closed house. In this regard, the watchman is the first of the play's Cassandras, if you understand by Cassandra the figure who sees ahead of time. And since as Valéry says "it takes faith to see . . . what *is*," both watchman and prophet have a problem with the faith of their listeners, their listeners' inability to believe in an unlikely truth.

The true is so routinely, so officially converted into the likely, the future into the foregone, the resumed into the presumed, the present into the prejudicial—that we need watchmen just to remind us to see what *is*. In his alertness, he can keep the past from passing out of mind: he knows what happened in the human house before, when brother turned on brother. In Aeschylus's play, this fraternal infidelity means the story of Atreus and Thyestes, whose mutual betrayal and revenge started the curse on their house. But there is always the antecedent fraternal betrayal in the house of human histories: those first brothers who invented human murder. It is a fundamental of the human story: the worst atrocities occur between the closest relatives.

There are those, like the chorus (that repository of convention), who know what *may* be said, and there are those others, like the watchman, who know what *can* be said. The watchman's job is not to invent but to convey what is visible. He does by sharpened sight and a trained eye what Cassandra does by virtue of a gift from the Gods. But the curse of the gift for her is that no one wants to believe her, while the watchman is expected to foresee the unexpected. His listeners need him, and he needs them in return: he can spread the word only if they can hear. (This is where the temporal paradox arose: if there is a gap anywhere ahead in the circuit, the current won't start down the wire.) Prophesy is a notoriously lonely art, but communication can't occur without community: an open, understanding, overseeing house . . .

I might add at this point that I take the artist to be a combination of the watchman and Cassandra, the trained and the inspired, the social and the alien, the wished for and the rebuffed. Aeschylus needs more than one figure to represent himself.

So the watchman presents the act of representing itself: he establishes the frame, the curtain, the sign of the scene. He is the eyes not only for the community of characters he serves, but for the audience too; and he opens a door onto the unfamiliar, the foreign, a door which cannot close until the play's end. In *Agamemnon*, that door will close about corruption at the heart of the familiar, and the house will turn out to be a destructively private place, the house of narrow self-construction, narrow-mindedness, the house closed off from others, home of hiding, seat of misrepresenting, house of horrors . . .

In *Agamemnon* the prophet is an unfamiliar figure, an alien, a foreigner. Cassandra is "unfamiliar" in more than one sense: unlike Clytemnestra she has had no child; she is without family. She was seized as a slave into a new land and household. Yet she will prove to be the truest figure in the play, while the usual familiars (husband, wife, parent and child, aunt and nephew) wind up housing the play's essential horror.[10] They lie to each other. They murder with love on their lips. The unbelievable is not so far off as we think (in this play the foreigner is telling the truth): the unbelievable, what we cannot take in or comprehend is, as Nietzsche knows, as Rilke knows, as Valéry knows, often uncomfortably close to home. What Freud says about the "uncanny"—in German, *unheimlich* or un-homelike—is apposite here: it's not the utterly strange or unidentifiable that scares us most, it is the streak of the familiar in it. Pointing up the familiar in the alien and the alien in the familiar, Aeschylus's *Agamemnon* demonstrates Nietzsche's contention that

It was artists, and especially those of the theater, who gave people eyes and ears . . . and taught us the art of viewing ourselves as heroes—from a distance . . . the art of staging and watching ourselves. Only in this way can we get over some base details in ourselves. Without this art we would be nothing but foreground, and live entirely in the spell of that perspective which makes what is closest at hand . . . appear as if it were vast, and reality itself. (*The Gay Science*, 78)

Perhaps the central questions in *Agamemnon*: What is other? What is unsayable? How is saying betrayed?

The tragedy of the ending of *Agamemnon* is figured partly in the closing-in of self-appointment around the self, for when Clytemnestra and her husband's murdering nephew (her new lover) go inside, and the door closes on that house, a larger social hope closes. The greatest violations, the greatest moral disorders, now called by the name of a new "order," get bedded into the family (where to society's detriment but by society's permission they may, after all, legally multiply). The parallels between *Agamemnon* and *Hamlet* (parallels which begin with the watchman and include the "rest is silence") go on to comprehend the horror of the corrupted intimate; the rotten state whose bodily part is the family and whose fate is bound up in the incestuous consequences of self-love; the self's incapacity to know that it comprehends—and to see that it embraces—the other. "Here we are again," wrote Valéry, "with the problem: the *other* vs. the *one*. That is, the chemical combination "like/unlike" . . . to which I . . . was led by an analysis of language" (II, 297).

Indeed, all language, were we to register its dramatizing act, does stage this play of alien and familiar. It cannot speak of itself without separating from itself; when language tries to contain (or represent) itself, it runs into spatial, temporal, and ontological problems. The problem of itself, for language, is it must treat itself as an other. (The first person, like the present moment, runs into difficulties in representation.) Speaking of language, one speaks in language; one is already two or three. The watchman opens the play, then leaves the scene to watch us watch. The author has always foreseen our seeing. His foresight persists, and becomes (itself) a figure in the reiterative "presence" of performance.

A literary work invariably involves some freak of time: from the author's point of view it is a present that will repeat, and from the audience's point of view it is something already done that is about to begin. The watchman leaves the scene. And only then the chorus enters, that witness most capable of witlessness, the witness who, though least likely to lie, is most likely to be mistaken. We, somewhere in the vicinity of these seers and watchers and witnesses—we onlookers—have our work cut out for us. *Incipit tragoedia.*

II

Monsieur Teste's companion describes Monsieur Teste at the opera. Where a work of art occurs, what its site is, bears some thought: the root of the word opera *is* work; its kin is *oeuvre*. Valéry locates us at the site of the works, and places M. Teste, as presiding intellect, above the body of the attending crowd. Once this altitude is established, then Teste, and the narrator, and the crowd and (even) Valéry and we, *all* work as forms of audience. But what is the work or oeuvre most central in all these regards? What work are we looking at? The same one Teste is looking at? Is Teste's mind central or circumstantial here? Is the act of the opera (that of composer? or librettist?) the point, and its status as oeuvre? Is it Valéry's art we most attend to? I maintain, thanks to Valéry's care, it is the work *of audience itself* that settles at the center of these aims and eyes: we, as audience onto Valéry, he as audience onto M. Teste; Teste as audience onto the crowd (the house the actors melt away into at the end of the spectacle); and the crowd as audience onto the operatic fiction—these forms of audience *become* the scene in this Valéry vista. (They are no longer relegated to the status of the off- or ob-scene.) Such circles of authority make *us* the point: the philosophical subject become a literary object.

But let us look at Teste. In the words of his companion at the Opera:

> He looked only at the audience. He was breathing the great burst of brilliance at the edge of the pit. He was red.
>
> An immense copper girl separated us from a group murmuring beyond the dazzlement. Deep in the vapor glittered a naked bit of woman, smooth as a stone. A number of ladies' fans were independently alive over the crowd, dark and bright, foaming up to the top lamps. My eyes spelled dozens of small faces, alighted on a sad head, rippled over bare arms, over people, and finally flickered out.
>
> Everyone was in his seat, free to make a slight movement. I had a taste for the system of classification, the almost theoretical simplicity of the audience, the social order. I had the delightful sensation that all that breathed in this cube would follow its laws, flare up in great circles, grow excited in sections; feel in groups things that were intimate—unique—secret stirrings, rising to the unavowable! I strayed over those layers of people, row by row, in orbits, fancying that I could bring together ideally all those with the same illness, or the same theory, or the same vice . . . One music touched us all; it swelled and then became quite small . . . (VI, 14–15).

In *étages* (translated here as "layers") we feel the cognate force of "stages": in the very language (of origin and of translation) we sense the staging of the audience itself. Valéry's attention is on the theater of the mind: the attention that usually operates as invisible narrator or framer of our experience now becomes the object of its own industry.

It is the disengagement of Valéry's attention that most amazes a reader —the unseduced coolness with which the eye is free to wander pointlessly, unhooked by particulars, by the sad head, for example, where an ordinary poet would have stopped and dwelled. Valéry isn't hooked by the urge to narrative, to develop a story attached to individual destinies. Elsewhere he says of his art: "This sensation of the multiplication of possibilities, very strong in me, has always turned me away from narration; and I regard the streams that flow from others with the admiration of a man for whom the contemplation and analysis of a glass of water are quite sufficient to absorb his time and curiosity" (II, 88).

The trail of regards in the Teste-at-opera passage seems sequential without being consequential: Valéry is watching not the conventional "sights" but rather the seeing itself. As a result, there is a kind of simultaneous motion-and-coolness to this looking-through-looking. The opera that interests Teste (and Valéry, writer of the text, and the third observer, the speaker *in* the text) is not the operatic story, not the fictive interior, the plot that captures the audience's attention and for which they *suspend* their disbelief. Like all great skeptics, Valéry *delights*, rather, *in* his disbelief. Follow the objects of this passage's vagrant gaze, a gaze which seems to go projecting out from the figure of one of the observers at the opera. The gaze's pace and idiosyncrasies reveal more about a seeing's habits than about a scene's objects, until finally what is clearest is a vision's motion (you could say its form of discontent), rather than any particular *content*. Not only are the objects of the gaze constantly shifting, but its own securing in a home ground also seems in question. Close and red *is Teste*, seen by the narrator; but then immense and copper is the girl in Teste's view, standing as she does beyond Teste, between the us (of Teste and narrator) and the them (of the distant group); then we (she, Teste, the narrator and we the readers too, of course) can see a group in the distance, a bit of a body, a thousand faces, a sad head, arms and people. Presented in rapid succession, this series of nouns is an extremely odd sequence or juxtapositive cluster, its scale so sliding as to destabilize the conventions of intellectual (or literary) progression. The noun-trail (a kind of thinging) passes from a group of bodies to a part of a body, then back to the level of the multiple, then to a head with meaning in it (it is sad). But the gaze does not rest on meaning, where most fictions sink their hook. The settlement Valéry speaks of ("settled on a sad head") is only temporary, a passing selection, not a staying; for the sentence now runs on with greater and greater speed and urgency—along arms, over people, and out. I "spelled" these things, says the English version, literalizing the French *épeler*. (In French, *épeler* is barely a vowel away from *appeller*, to name or call.) "Spelled" is, in the English, all the richer for suggesting not only lettering, that founding arbitrariness of literary orders, but also spells of the kind that can be cast, and of the kind that can be spent, in times and turns of dwelling.

Oddities climax in Valéry's list when he reaches the word "people": people are the final element in this list. Other elements were odd enough in their sequence and pacing, but this is odd in its order of magnitude: it includes the whole in a list of parts, as yet another part. In this way it draws our attention to the taxonomic act itself, and the upheaval of our ordinary orders of interpretation.[11] Look where the line of vision comes to rest. "Flickered out" brings us back to the eyes from which we were first launched: what flickers out is not merely an object, but an attention; both are extinguished at once.

The coolness of this regard is Valéry's resistance to prefiguration, to the prejudicial narratives of storytelling, time, and language itself. If you read his little piece about the newborn art of motion pictures ("The Screen," in *Poems in the Rough*) you begin to understand how for him all projection is mental: "Actions are speeded up or slowed down. Their order may be reversed. The dead revive and laugh . . . Everyone can see with his own eyes that all that is, is surface . . . Finally, by means of stills and close-ups, the act of attention is itself represented."[12] What the artist's eye then comes to rest on is the husk or device of consciousness itself: the subject become its own object, self saying self, saying saying saying . . . Beckett will drive the resultant aporia to its ineluctable end: "whenever said said said missaid" (*Worstward Ho*).

What I call "coolness of regard" is a modernist trait. In Valéry, it amounts to a kind of respect: a resistance to the habit of interpretation by which the instrument disappears in the service of a reference. It takes the form of a persistence in the study of appearance, a willingness to let perceptual phases and transformations take (and give) place: no predisposition to a settlement, no forecast heaven to arrive at. (Valéry elsewhere says, eternity is motionless. Perhaps that is the trouble with eternity; for the life is the living, and its means, like those of the work of art, are moving.)

Surprise contains the prize as the event of the actual already contains, implied, the eventuality of the *déjà vu*. (The present begins, after all, in a pre-.) Valéry's looking seems less intentive or retentive than attentive. He pays attention, patiently, without immediately stowing away evidence into standard or pre-emptive mental slots. Freed from conventions of affect and standards of disposing judgment, Valéry can cause the orders of looking itself ("I had a taste for the system of classification") to form part of the scene, an attention to attention's taxonomies, tastes, and tests.

Like Nietzsche and Rilke, Valéry has contracted the modernist disease. Bedeviled by the paradox of mind having only itself to know itself with, he is drawn to the question of differentiation: between self and other, continuity and interruption, now and then, same and different, where do we draw the defining line?—even, for example, the line around being, the placement of which is that question that Heidegger insists underlies and subsumes all questions. Consequently we must ask not only: What are we calling being?, but also (perhaps more fundamentally, if you wish to play the Heideggerian language-game): What are we calling calling? The question leads itself into uncontainabilities of echo.

III

Nietzsche's *The Gay Science* originally ended on the words with which his subsequent work, *Zarathustra*, would begin. (A later edition buried the end in the middle.) Interesting to ponder the successive architectures of such designing, to study the space of ideas the way Valéry did the ideas of space. (Well before Bachelard wrote his *Poetics of Space*, Valéry was playing with ideas of architecture AS architecture of ideas—was interested in such spaces as the cubicle, the cave, the tomb.)

The *Untergang* of Zarathustra both ends *The Gay Science* and begins the subsequent (and eponymous) book. It is anticipated in the former by Latin and German forms of the phrase "The tragedy begins." If the tragedy is said to begin as of the end of one work and the beginning of another, where can we place this tragedy, in literary terms?

If the tragedy begins at the end, does it reside after words? (That is, outside language?) But if another work *begins* with Zarathustra's Untergang, then the tragedy must also *follow* to unfold *in* language. And what, anyway, is *in* or *out* of language? What is in or out of *mind*?[13] If, as Valéry claims to do, one can watch oneself, can mind one's mind—not to dominate, but to describe—then does one stand outside oneself, beside oneself? *Go out to come in*, says the sign over the portal in Valéry's mythical Xiphos. But it's easier said than done, and Nietzsche goes on to say:

How far the perspectival character of existence extends or indeed whether existence has any other character; whether existence without interpretation, without "sense," does not become "nonsense"; whether, on the other hand, all existence is not essentially an interpretive existence—that cannot be decided even by the most industrious and most scrupulously conscientious analysis and self-examination of the intellect; for in the course of this analysis the human intellect cannot avoid seeing itself in its own perspectives, and *only* in these. We cannot look around our own corner . . . (GS #374, Kaufmann tr., modified)

Valéry's response is that there is plenty (maybe an endlessness) *within* our corner we fail to see: the mystery is in sight. For much of modern philosophy, all consciousness is self-consciousness. Valéry's other, like Nietzsche's, is most of all self.

"And how many people," asks Nietzsche, "know how to observe something! And of the few who do, how many observe themselves? 'Everybody is farthest away—from himself'; all who try the reins know this to their chagrin, and the maxim 'know thyself,' addressed to human beings by a god, is almost malicious" (GS #335). Yet "we want to become who we are"—and the regard by which this might be possible must restore to the word "regard" its dispassion. It is in order to see clearly that Nietzsche wishes to suspend the story of good and evil, the customary placement of the lines, the privileges of an inherited way of seeing. How can one look unflinchingly, he wonders, at WHAT IS, if some prior SHOULD BE is altering the evidence? To look at, in the old French, had "guard" at heart; the closest watcher was the keeper.

Here is Valéry in that regard:

A Charitable Attention

What a number of things you have not even *seen*, in this street you travel six times daily, in this room where you spend so many hours a day! Look at the angle between those planes of bookcase and window. Always visible, in vain it has long cried for vision—to be somehow rescued—and you must *save* it—afford it what your arrested sensibility has until now derivatively lavished upon the paltriest sublime prospect, sunset, storm at sea, museum exhibit, or whatever. All that looking is ready-made. But spare something for this poor wretch of a corner, this workaday hour and surroundings, and you will be repaid a hundredfold. (II, 78–79)

This, like much of Valéry's prose-poetry, insists: no detail is insignificant: it is significant as a sign of itself or of sensing, itself: there is a sheer joy in the bound and boundlessness of *the perceived ordinary*—he refuses the *received* sublime.

When Nietzsche defends himself against charges that he is incomprehensible (for working in glimpses, flashes, aphoristic snips) he says,

There are truths that are singularly shy and ticklish and cannot be caught except suddenly—truths that must be surprised or left alone . . . What you are about to hear is new; if you do not understand it, if you misunderstand the singer . . . that happens to be "the singer's curse." (GS #381, #383)

In such a proclamation one hears the words of Aeschylus's watchman at work. (Nietzsche modifies the "singer's curse" with a devil-may-care "what does it matter": the gesture agrees with his science's gaiety but there is ample evidence of Nietzsche's concern with the obtuseness of his "house.") As a matter of professional care, the artist must find surprising what most people take for granted. The record that is his work is no mere mechanism; it must accomplish (as evidence and grounds for successive takings-to-heart) the first time (the unexpected), and it must do so again and again. Asks Nietzsche,

What is it that the common people take for knowledge? . . . Nothing more than this: something strange is to be reduced to something familiar . . . What is familiar means . . . that we no longer marvel at it . . . How easily . . . men of knowledge are satisfied! . . . for "what is familiar is what is known," on this they are agreed. Even the most cautious among them suppose that what is familiar is at least more easily knowable than what is strange and that, for example, sound method demands that we start from the "inner world," from the "facts of consciousness," because this world is more familiar to us. Error of errors! . . . What we are used to is most difficult to "know"—that is, to see as a problem; that is, to see as strange, as distant, as "outside us." (GS #355)

Nietzsche's capacity, like Valéry's—and like Cassandra's, too—is to look unflinchingly at what others would dismiss or overlook or turn away from; and the wave patterns of that attention are their signatures as artists.

✳

An epigraph from Henri de la tour d'Auvergne opens the final book of *The Gay Science*: "Carcasse, tu trembles? / Tu tremblerais davantage, si / tu savais, ou je te mene." ("You tremble, carcass? You would tremble more if you knew where I was taking you.") Turenne (like other vicomtes, he is known by the name of his territory) was speaking as a general, but might as well be speaking as a poet or philosopher. In any case, he is speaking as that part of a man that places itself above, thus outside, the carcass. He is speaking *to* his body, which his address suggests may not go on without him. Is the reverse true? Can *he* go on without *it*? We fear not; that is why "you would tremble more if you knew" should make *us* tremble: he is speaking to himself. He knows and does not know what will happen to him, and the half that knows is talking to the half that does not know. This is exactly our relation to our own death: half ignoring, half remembering. And carcass is already a dead body: Turenne is addressing his own mortality. Nietzsche takes this text for epigraph because it reveals a sensibility able to bear what *must be*. In general, the mind cannot bear it; the mind flinches, turns away from death. The body, by contrast, we think, can not. But as Valéry says, "What I see blinds me. What I hear deafens me. What I know with renders me ignorant" (VI, 36). He resembles Nietzsche in his yearning for an open, an unprejudiced, a welcoming consciousness (an *amor fati*). In place of the old ideals and icons (knowledge, unity, the expected, the convention, the ideal) both writers love change, surprise, multiplicity, centerlessness. Nietzsche writes,

We cannot see around our own corner: it is a hopeless curiosity that wants to know what other kinds of intellects and perspectives there *might* be; for example, whether some beings might be able to experience time backward, or alternately forward and backward (which would involve another direction of life and another concept of cause and effect). But I should think that today we are at least far from the ridiculous immodesty involved in decreeing from our corner that perspectives are permitted only from this corner. Rather has the world become "infinite" for us all over again, inasmuch as we cannot reject the possibility *that it may include infinite interpretations* (GS #374)

The new infinity differs from the old one in being an assertion not of the dimension of the single monolithic text (or scripture) but of the multiplicity of readings. If, further, the reader takes himself for text, the unknowability deepens rather than diminishes. *Dasein* is, as Heidegger says, the site of the *openness* of being.

Valéry asks, Who is more a stranger than he who notes himself seeing what he sees? and then observes: "the strangeness of things . . . when this feeling comes over me I recognize myself"; and, "a body strangely endowed with the past—an imminence, an implex, an aside, an oddity, a blank: my Self" (II, 240; 277; 284). But modernists are not the first to yearn to admit otherness back in to the self-styled self, to reclaim the alias or alien from its categorical remove.

In their studies of studies, their inquiries into questions of distinction-making, of identifying (sameness-making)—optical, reflective, reflexive —Nietzsche and Valéry may seem to make an icon out of the clasm, a necro out of the phile: I think rather they ask us to reunderstand what we hold sacred, to wake "from habit itself." We write in time: and though the time of the timeless ideal has given way to a fashion of chance, of flaw's fatality, nevertheless time's current is alternating: a flame and a worry, a flourish and wane. It comes and it goes: as Plato says, we owe the god of health a sacrifice.

(Or was it Socrates who said it? Socrates was *said* to have said it— one of Derrida's themes in *The Postcard* involves this recurrent question: in the *Dialogues*, who's whose mouthpiece? Given that we have of Socrates nothing but representations by others, and of Plato nothing but transcripts of Socratic thought—given that their mutual dependence is by now almost perfect, and both are treated by history as their history's author, how could we decide of the two which is the self, and which the other?) Socrates beguiles these guys. He appears in the dialogues of Valéry, in the dallyings of Derrida; Nietzsche mulls (or rakes) him over. Hermeneuts love him: he is representation's very representative. He is the story of intellect, a twice removed figure, the soul of the soul; he is the thought of someone else, he is someone's self and everyone's other. His inquiry into the particulars of the death he's about to undergo has the coolness of a brave regard not unrelated to the enterprise of a writer like Valéry: ask yourself who is the you, in Valéry's little poem "You Forget":

> You forget, but your body persists . . .
> You see, and it does not.

You walk, it stamps its feet.
You taste and it digests,
You smile and it wrinkles.
You sleep and it sleeps.

It did not know that you were changing your mind.
You did not know that it was changing its might, down there in the depths.

(II, 244)

Between you and it, the gestures seesaw. And don't you, despite yourself, find yourself thinking the "you" is *really* the mind and the "it" *merely* the body? Don't we make ourselves, to some extent, a little image of ourselves, a person behind our eyes, in our head? How did mind so divorce itself from body, that the body became the mind's third person, and the mind its own second?

Look at the paired gestures in the poem—note how some seem causal, some simultaneous; notice the balance of comparison to contrast, how the first two pairs clearly set up a pattern of contrast, but the third ("you walk and it stamps its feet") could be said to be rather a resemblance, perhaps an obedience or imitation on the body's part. (However, because the two preceding instances so stressed the body's resistance, we tend to highlight the distinctions thereafter in the pairs, in which case "stamps its feet" takes on a certain petulance or tantrum aspect; "stamps its feet" can thus be said to add either impediment or energy to the will to walk, depending on your slant.) The flavor and shadings of comparison get subtler with "you taste and it digests" (here we tend to draw the distinction between aesthete and mechanic), and in "you smile and it wrinkles"—intention followed by inscription, the body making the mind's mood written, and thus relatively (ironically) enduring. Yet again there is an intimation of rebellion—a wrinkle of distaste in response to the smile, a wrinkle of revenge: what it wrinkles, after all, is you! In sleep there is identity between them, apparent identity. But "You sleep and it sleeps" by now has an ominous shadow, because the breather cannot sleep, unless it is dead. And last but most, in the not-knowing each bears the other, the changes (in one of mind, in the other of might) begin to augur greater powers than either alone or both together can keep up. The power to die is, after all, self-extinguishing.

Elsewhere Valéry writes, as if about the construction of a ship (he is talking partly about the act of art in which he is engaged): "no architecture can be more subtle than that which erects upon the movable a construction which is the mover and the moved . . ." If one had to choose, between body and mind, which were the mover and which the moved, one finally couldn't. The ambiguity's important . . . The old safe grounds, sacred grounds, have fallen away; it is the movable we must be premised on: the sea for Valéry is a figure of that *Abgrund* (abyss) Nietzsche insists we must not turn away from. The Unmoved is dead, to rephrase the modernist slogan; and Valéry and Nietzsche are entering the age of the science of uncertainty, the science of matter seen as energy itself. The mover and the moved cannot be disentangled; neither can the body and the mind. It is because Valéry can't tell subject and object apart, because he is so absorbed in his objects and so removed from his subject, because, in short, of a ferocious kind of love—that he so frequently seems so non-committal, casting about for many (not only seeking the one), and constantly doing research in the realm of Rimbaud's "Je *est* un autre." There are two persons in "You Forget," two halves of self, but they are the second and the third: where is the first? If the poem brings anything home, it brings home something alien (as did Agamemnon the king): the farthest out of the third persons, the least familiar. It's an it, this *alter tuus*. If you *are* your mind (the overseer, ego or superego), then *it* (the undertaker, the body) is the one who takes you down. Whichever way you look at it, there is no *one*, no first person, no single self. An other is always built-in. It is hard to think of yourself thinking, Valéry reminds us (though he does it all the time): but it is impossible to think of the thinker of you thinking. Inconceivable, the third remove. We are two from the first, two at once.

We cannot (ever, but especially as readers) see ourselves, but reciprocity arises out of the thought of the seen *seeing back*, and making us its object, so a kind of imaginative triangulation obtains. The division of pronouns into three persons arises out of this act of imaginative equation. But the equation is never realized, for the first person is deeply unlike the second and third, different in its very (and comprehensive) premising (just as the present's category is constitutively different from those of the past and the future). Still we tend to think of the three persons available to us in grammar as somehow equally dividing up the range of actual person-relations. The leaps we falsely assume equal (leaps from self to second person, and from second to third) are analogous to the counterpart numerical leaps: the differences between zero and one, one and two, two and three are quantitatively but not qualitatively alike. Compared to them, all the subsequent intervals are virtually equivalent. One could say that all the quandaries and subtleties of philosophical reflection on reflexion arise in the relations among nothing, one, two and three, and (in our registration of these relations) the serial distortion of the ordinal into the cardinal.

In French the paradox of the one-as-other (and the first-as-third person) is powerfully, linguistically apparent (we have a trace of it in the pronoun "one" one sometimes uses in English to mean oneself: a first-person meaning, but a third person pronoun). *On* in French is much more clearly than in English a first-person substitute; in fact, it is frequently translated as "I" or "we." Valéry plays on this first-person-alien in the dream transcription we find in *Poems in the Rough*:

> *One* is at sea, lying in a bunk; two bodies in one; narrowly joined, and one wonders whether one or two, because of this constriction of the exiguous bed of the cabin. This onefold and twofold creature is prey to an infinite sadness, a pain and tenderness that is *with him*, without limits or cause. A storm wind howls in the night outside. The ship rolls and groans terribly. Creature latches to creature and *one* is aware of the anguished beating of a single heart, the dull thuds of the engine thumping and struggling with the sea, the regular poundings, ever more violent, of the raging waves upon the hull.
>
> Terror, danger, tenderness, anguish, the yawing, the force of the waves, grow to a *breaking point*.
>
> And at last the catastrophe is come. The hatches give way, the very wall parts, spewing deadly water.
>
> I wake. *My face is bathed in tears.* They have rolled down my cheeks, to my lips, and my first sensation is the taste of their salt, which doubtless has just evoked this whole desperate complex of tenderness, sorrow, and sea. (II, 161–62; Valéry's italics)

Reading as a grammatical crafter, I admire the economies of this *on* (or "one"), that is, its doubleness: for it acts both as the word for a singleness *and* as the third person pronoun that splits it toward the alien. Onefold and twofold, this *on* is the dreamt and the dreamer, the self and the seer, the self and the sayer—in dream as in the languages of waking. The breaking point is at the separation of dreamer from dreamt: the dreamt one dies, the dreaming one wakes up and then becomes *an other*—perhaps in yet another dream, a dream we think of as reality. In this ensuing reality there is salt water on his face. And if, as he says, the tears have provoked the sea-dream, then the effect of sorrow somehow precedes the cause. Once again we have what Nietzsche calls the "untimeliness" of an acute sensitivity: it is Cassandra's sorrow before the fact.

But what I find most striking in this event's description is its perfect parallel to that of a childbirth seen from the inside. The intimated other is surrounding but confining—look at Valéry's choice of terms: two bodies in one, narrowly joined, constriction of the bed of the cabin; the pain and tenderness that is *with* him; the ship groaning, the engine thumping, the regular poundings . . . These all strike me as evocative of labor; this hold and intimated other is the mother in whom he is immersed; at the breaking point the two-in-one must make two *out* of one, for "the very wall parts" and then he wakes, wet, to another world. Post-partum, he says "My first sensation is the taste of . . . salt." No longer identified as *one*, but now as *I*, having a face to be bathed, he has *become* an other. He owns a face, he has a self: indeed, he *is* it, a person you'd have to call the third.

IV

Among Valéry's dialogues, the one entitled "Colloquy Within a Being" makes the instability of a unitary self explicitly its subject. (Once, in Valéry's notebooks, Teste the character speaks up, as if independent, telling Valéry to change the meter of a poem.) "Colloquy Within a Being" records a discourse between the A and B of a single self awaking in the morning; A exhorts B to rise, B resists, and A tells B, "You are going to differ from yourself as a slack rope differs from that selfsame rope when taut."

The selfsame differs. Thus "the Self" as constituted begins to fall apart, in the manner of those other lost unities (God, Truth, et al.). It turns into only *a* self, no longer definite in its article; no longer one's own or only, but one among many, some of them born, some made. And how is a self made? Like other entities (all entities are suspected of being verbal, after Heidegger) it is marked out, first; it is a matter of drawing the lines. The aged Valéry, assembling pieces from his career for a book called *Mixture*, complained (with relish): "This is an old man's problem: he knows very well that he is the *same*, but he would be hard put to provide convincing proof of this little proposition. The 'I' is perhaps no more than a convenient symbol, as empty as the verb 'to be'—both technical terms, the more convenient for being empty" (II, 313).

So we could say one way of drawing the self is to draw a zero: What does it contain? What does it exclude? The German language makes infinitive (*Sein*) what English makes participial (being); in either case you add an article and the ongoing turns into a shortcoming: a verb of indefinite extension becomes a noun of limits.

But where is *being* being kept? Heidegger finds its ground eroded, from the etymological/ontological first. Being is empty, he says. Yet we have this sense of being as completing, as *fait accompli*; becoming is the one that is never done. Being and becoming seem in this way temporally distinct: what *is* "resists every onsurge of becoming."[14] If being is defined as what gathers to it the unchanged, the full and permanent, that is, if being is the done; and at the same time if Heraclitus is right (everything is in flux), then there *is* nothing *but* becoming, no being but being coming un- . . .

As for appearances (which contemporary speakers think deceptive, or as something to be "kept up") they were once the *root* of being. For the Greek sense of appearance as being was traceable to the word "radiance." (As Heidegger tracks it back, what was said to *be* was what stood up in the light and thus, literally, appeared.) Nowadays the synonym for appearance is semblance, and semblance (unlike resemblance) has some air of false faith about it.[15]

Heidegger tells us that the shining of appearance-as-emergence became (in due morphological time) the dimming of appearance-as-semblance; seeming seemed increasingly *opposed* to (rather than identified with) being. By the time of the Sophists and Plato, appearance had become *mere* appearance, and the real was removed to on high, to be Being, an exalted idea, suprasensory; while life (below) was degraded into semblance. The early Christians then inherited this phenomenal cosmology, and passed it on to us. Heidegger chooses Sophocles to illustrate the struggle between being and appearance in classical Greece (see his *Introduction to Metaphysics*, pp. 106ff). We can see for ourselves how central this struggle is in *Agamemnon*.

Cassandra is blessed with the knowledge of the truth of the future, and (thus) cursed with consequences: no one will believe her when she tells it. Given appearances (how suspect some are, how important it is to keep others up, given the institutional orders, out of whose temporal and legal limits women, for example, must not leap) the representations made by the two women become mortally important to the dynamics of *Agamemnon*.

At the play's very outset, after the watchman does his doubletalk and disappears, Clytemnestra tries in vain to convince the Chorus she has received a message (by relays of beacons). Twice the chorus fails to believe her true understanding about the fall of Troy. So here we have a foretaste of Cassandra's dilemma. And although Clytemnestra and Cassandra are antagonists in action, Clytemnestra's relation to Cassandra inscribes a resemblance. Representations, like appearances, have a double sense: on the one hand as *reiterations* they can be faithful, on the other as *claims* they can be—and are suspected to be—false; this difference within sameness constitutes the narrative engine of the play. "The future you shall know when it has come," say the chorus early in the play; "before then, forget it."

What is unspeakable about the future is death, and a *memento mori* is a memory of something not yet experienced. Women are mistaken, says the representative of moderation and of reason (the chorus) because they tend to leap out of time, are "too quick to shift from ground to ground." (Memory, persistence, ritual all enforce rationality's cultural and political institutions: but in this play such powers as monarchy and family will prove false.)

The chorus, so worried about false appearances, misses the true when the true does shine. Having twice been told by Clytemnestra what news she has gleaned from the beacon relays, the chorus nevertheless doesn't know what to think until the official messenger approaches: "Now," says the cautious Chorus, "we shall understand these torches and their shining . . . They may be real; yet bright and dreamlike ecstacy in light's appearance might have charmed our hearts away . . ." (It is no accident that this fear of being deceived sounds so much like a fear of love, and that a woman was the bearer of the suspect signs.) The chorus cannot accept a truth that comes along an unaccustomed path; it cannot accept anything *out of order* . . . Later it will be clear Clytemnestra had been telling the truth about the battle's outcome; and one of the ironies of the drama consists in the chorus's disbelief when she is telling the truth, and its later credulity when she lies. There is something of the Cretan paradox in this; after the second (and mis-) representation, Clytemnestra will declare herself a liar, and be telling the truth again.

Literary theorists are fond of pointing out, these days, that the whole institution of language operates to some extent along Cretan-liar lines: a statement is always implicitly both referring outside itself, and remaining a statement about itself: it says it IS the truth it is indicating, but the act of indication, like a pointing finger, always points away. In a sense, all statements occur (implicitly) in quotes. The quotes, missing, are nevertheless in effect, and refer to the act of reference. These implicit quotes around acts of statement mean: "This statement is true." Representation, as force and failure both, is itself represented by that missing sign. Our gullibility, taking the world of words for the real world, is that of consciousness: it cannot imagine what cannot be said. The saying itself lights up the seen.

When Clytemnestra does her ceremonial lying as the good wife welcoming Agamemnon home near the end of the play, the chorus applauds her, because the ceremony itself is conventional, and reassures the chorus. Like most rituals, it provides a buffer against something which threatens unity or sanity: in this case, it reassures the chorus that no death is coming, despite the prophecies. Clytemnestra lies and the chorus commends her: these are "words that impress interpreters," they say. *Their* interpretive function is to reinforce or secure convention: the chorus is of standard-bearers, conservatives; they represent the inertial force of mores, of prevailing interpretation, and it is in them, in their mistakes of understanding, in their downfall (the downfall, so to speak, of the audience represented within the play), that the play makes its subtlest political point.

We misrepresent things TO OURSELVES. "I think this strange girl needs some interpreter," says the chorus when Cassandra will not speak. And yet it's rather that the chorus cannot hear: it can't hear the message about death—every time the fatal future is hinted at, the chorus recoils, calling the subject unspeakable. The senses of the chorus have already been shaped by the permissible. This is the condition imposed by social life: the sensual cannot speak out except as the consensual, and our imminent (and individual) deaths cannot faze the body of social meaning and social life, cannot (literally) be comprehended. The truth of death is always just beyond us, cannot sink in, not least because we cannot bear to believe it. Cassandra is, like the artist, the person who must bear, who must believe, who—out of the order of convention, out of the order of time—must suffer the end in advance.

There is a stunning exchange after the conquered Cassandra is brought, in the carriage of Agamemnon, to Clytemnestra's door. Repeatedly instructed by Clytemnestra to alight and come into the house, Cassandra knows Clytemnestra is about to murder Agamemnon and then Cassandra herself: she foresees her own death. She does not alight; she does not speak. In her persistent silence we recognize a terrible understanding, but Clytemnestra hears only obstinacy, barbarian ignorance, vacancy. Later Cassandra will say "I know Greek far too well"; and to us her silence speaks volumes. (It is useful to remember at this juncture Valéry's piece on the varieties of silence—and Kant's on the varieties of nothing; both create taxonomies of absence.) In *Agamemnon* not only language but silence too can be wrongly interpreted: the chorus acts as a mistaken interlocutor, urging Cassandra to obey the express command of Clytemnestra, and Clytemnestra makes a last angry (and inadvertently preposterous) command: ". . . If in ignorance you fail to comprehend, speak not, but make with your barbarian hand some sign," the preposterousness of which command winds up making Clytemnestra laughable, not the outsider Cassandra. The failure to understand keeps redounding to the speaker's, not the listener's, discredit; that is why the watchman threatens to forget, should *we* fail him.

In exasperation at Cassandra's silence (that silence we know comes from knowing too much, not knowing too little—a sign not of the unsayable, but of the unspeakable), Clytemnestra retreats again into the house, and the chorus, while sympathizing with Cassandra, induces her to descend from the coach. That is when finally she utters something. But what she utters is an incomprehensible cry: otototoi popoi, she wails, bewailing language itself (Apollo!), you might say, for it is the curse of signs to leap out of the actual, to escape the limits of the present, to save the past and propose the future. Cassandra's curse *is* the curse of language, expressed in consciousness: I mean self-consciousness, whose object is its subject, and in whose duplications the conclusion is *always* foregone.[16]

"We want no prophets in this place," says the otherwise sympathetic chorus. "Art and multiplication of words drifting through tangled evil bring terror" to the hearer. And later, having heard the horrifying prophecy, the chorus still cannot say what it cannot see, cannot bear the unspeakable, even at the very threshold ("What terror whirls you backward from the door? . . . What foulness then, *unless some horror in the mind*?" [my italics]). Whereupon we hear Cassandra's last wish: "Bear witness to me when I die . . . here in my death I claim this stranger's grace of you." This is the *voice of what is particular* in the artist speaking to the *heart of what is general* in people: within any one of us, it is the petition we make to our ritual, usual, habitual, socialized selves. It is what private experience requires of public representation. The chorus, which is the audience within the play, is an accomplice. Its ignorance is no innocence, for it hears but does not listen. It sees but cannot look.

The chorus is the generality of men, the herd of which Nietzsche is so disdainful. Only when it hears Agamemnon twice cry out that he has been stabbed a deadly blow—only then does it believe. Immediately something happens, in the play's very structure, that feels to me fundamentally terrifying: the chorus—that representative of stability and unity, of the general opinion and moderated way—the chorus, that stand-in for us as a human group, the represented audience—the chorus itself suddenly and without warning *breaks up*. What had been until this moment so consistently a single, moderate, predictable voice fractures into many voices, chaotic, disunified, panic-stricken; suddenly it speaks as wild, undirected, numerous, nameless individuals. Until this moment it had been the univocal repository of mores and order, versed in customary signs; it was, like the southerners in Valéry's fictive island of Xiphos, forbidden "to teach what no one can know, or to publish anything whatever without proof." But now the chorus has to face a terrible truth, the act of murder and the fact of Clytemnestra's confession ("Much have I said before," she says, "to serve necessity, but I will take no shame now to unsay it all.") In this corruption of a representation the chorus experiences the loss of its own grounds, for the only acceptable future was a predictable one, a usual one, a conventional one; and the only acceptable speech a conforming.

In cases where the true state of affairs is unspeakable, even its representation on stage is not permitted. (The two bloody deaths occur out of sight, in the etymological home of the obscene.) The fact of the occurrence, the existence, of death (not only, I think, wrongful death) is the encircling fact of the play. The capacity of human beings to believe death imminent is the play's grounding concern. Now that the unspeakable—the unbearable, the unseen—has been proven true, the chorus has lost its grounds for unity, and conformity becomes deformity. They break up into individuals the moment death becomes actual for them. They have lost their grounds for faith (faith in words, in convention, in the timeliness of things). Sounding now like Cassandra crying "Ai ai ai, Apollo, Apollo," they moan "alas . . . a doom that shall never be done with, and all through Zeus, Zeus, first cause, prime mover." The difference is that they are crying it *after* the fact, while she *fore*felt it, but still there is a disorder in time—the first cause is author of an endless, beginningless doom. Thus can enforced amnesia ensue, a forgetting by fiat; this is a further disorder in time. The last words of the play are Clytemnestra's, as she urges Aegisthus not to battle the chorus but to accompany her back into the house. (Unlike Cassandra he obeys, perhaps because he is unable to foresee what further ill futures may lie there.) The play as a whole has described a long curve from outward-looking—the watchman studying the sky for signs from foreign lands—toward the last gesture's inturning, when the malefactors retreat into the house, there to embody the domestication of corruption. Clytemnestra says to Aegisthus, about the horrified chorus, "*Forget them*, dearest; you and I have the power; we two shall bring good order to our house at least." Good order! Such a definition robs words of meaning, such official terms will institute a government on a groundlessness, Nietzsche's *Abgrund*. In Lattimore's foregrounding of forgetting here, the forgotten future (a figure, really, of the forgotten past, when curses were incurred) turns to misbegotten present, and language itself keeps a hollow house.

Clytemnestra's murderous acts were, at least in part, motivated by her sorrow at Agamemnon's having murdered their child. (He called it a religious sacrifice, a calling that one could say is, itself, a ritual substitution.) Aeschylus's story as a whole is the story of the evasions, displacements, substitutions, and detours language affords the sayer: how the corruption of appearance and representation turn the true false, and the seer's radiance turns to the sayer's semblance.

V

The unsaid shapes itself in our imagination only at its boundary, where the said reaches its limits. To us the unsaid seems to surround the said and to extend endlessly outward from it. We feel that the said explies the unsaid, rather than implies it. Any poem, any work of art, negotiates this dubious relation. For part of the unsaid (that endless extent) is the world of non-words referred to by the said, a corresponding world, a matching world (just as for the extent of space there is thought to be a space of anti-matter, exactly matter's match). But we think of what surrounds as being bigger, by nature, than what it encloses; so intuitively we feel the unsaid is bigger than the said, and must contain not only the world to which the said refers, but more.

As soon as representation occurs, you have a freak of time: a second-able "present," a temporal oxymoron. Whatever remains unsayable (un-containable in the space of presentation or corral of representation) stays outside of time. A poet makes use of the fact that language need not *contain* in order to provoke, to spark, to elicit, or to chime, and the poet does this art of triggering not only with the resources of linguistic music (and its counterpart emotions in the listener) but also with the resources of the simultaneous.

If acts of poetry tend by nature toward what is out of orders of time, they tend too toward the silent. What is overt is not necessarily what is outspoken in a poem: some silences are overt. And what else is an open-ing, the overture, of a work, if not a promise of its other—something beyond opening (something, that is, opened)? Oeuvre, opera, umbrella: are they not the mechanisms of an opening, that opening (and closing) of which Heidegger says *Dasein* is the site?

Let us look at a linguistic trace, an essentially unidentifiable fragment, a little line that appeared as an unrelated note among the papers in the Nietzsche archives. (I refer you especially to Derrida's extraordinary read-ing of it, in *Spurs. Nietzsche's Styles.*)

The fragment appears in quotes, and seems to bear no relation to any of the more complete, more coherent papers among which it was found. The fragment is this: "I have forgotten my umbrella."

First it is worth considering the frame: the archive of the written, that daily place not only of completions but of notes, some of which develop into (and are found later, in backward order, to have preceded) works by which the author became known. Some notes remain undeveloped, or abortive; some are commentaries on the writer's own literary acts, re-minders, remainders . . . But this one is peculiar, in that it seems precisely not to refer to any literary or philosophical act, though it appears in the frame of such acts.

Its resistance to the frame of the author's fame (the archival setting) becomes, in its own way, a comment on audience and solitude—a provocation to his biographers and interpreters. (One can imagine Nietzsche imagining them imagining him . . . he was a proud and frame-shattering man.) He was also often mercilessly funny (though he is more often remembered for the mercilessness than the humor): to read Nietzsche is to read a blazing stylist, someone swinging from invective to confiding, from vituperations (at a *them*) to inveiglement (at a *you*) in the blink of an eye. He'd love the interpretive bedevilments which would ensue, in the archives, on the heels of such an authorial absconding. A funny footnote to this handnote is the fact that Freud considered the umbrella a particularly ambiguous structure in itself: phallic in its shaft, female in its folds. Unless you're a Bulgarian terrorist, you don't use it when it's closed: you have to open it. Its point is, in some degree, to lose its point. Only the English word continues to refer to a use to which it's never put: umbrella casts a shade only in sunlight, like a parasol: etymologically, both are made for sun. In German and in French, for example, the parasol-for-rain has its own name. Only in English does the opposite *remain* so folded up inside the word.

And what of Freud's citation of the Austrian joke: "A wife is like an umbrella . . ." (the aperture, the chasm, between the first and second lines of this joke is big enough for entire audiences to fall into). "A wife is like an umbrella," he says: "sooner or later one takes a cab." What isn't said is to the point here. One must imagine in what rains an umbrella is needed, and the greater rains requiring cabs; one must let the hint of the hired and the had, the public and the privately owned, pass through one's mind; one must consider what one carries, and what one is carried by; and one must imagine, further, the forgettability of the umbrella. It's a poignant, even painful, joke for wives to have to hear.

I am not forgetting the umbrella of Nietzsche. He shared a love with Freud, in many more ways than one. Finally he himself couldn't really forget the instrument (his testimony notwithstanding). And to my mind this is the crucial point: "I have forgotten my umbrella" can't be said until it isn't true any longer: the mind must have recalled it to *call* it at all. If the verb were "left" ("I have left my umbrella") or if the noun were not so precise an object ("I have forgotten something") then the paradox wouldn't arise. But the noun is most and memorably particular, and the verb is "forgotten," so the mind's own mazes get implicated. One remembers, in this connection, Heidegger's "Forgetfulness of being itself falling into forgetfulness." (*Introduction to Metaphysics*, p. 19). As Joyce put it, "Was he [Bloom] doubly irritated? Because he had forgotten and because he remembered that he had reminded himself not to forget" (*Ulysses* 17.78–79).

With the Nietzsche fragment, we have a cousin to the paradox of the *memento mori* (that remembering of what has not yet happened): "I have forgotten my umbrella" is an announcement of one's own forgetting which is able to occur only after the forgetting is over. In a sense this is a cousin to the paradox implicit in all writings: their *now* evaporates immediately, but their traces persist. This is why I think the quotation marks *are* the point(s), in this note. The quotes point to the act of language itself, a claim within which we can't be true. The saying itself undoes it. What we have again is a paradox of the order of the Cretan liar. Saying in its very grounding refers us back to a linguistic incapacity, and to limitations even on our consciousness. We have forgotten, at any time, more than we know.

So we are back with Valéry, who insists, "How many things under our very eyes are invisible! Even on the retina they are still as unperceived as if they did not exist . . ." (II, 280). With Valéry, whose records of a world of sensory flux are so cool, we are not subject to passionate catharses. Valéry doesn't take looks to *care*, he takes care to look. He is not looking *at* a world, he is looking *as* it.

Valéry is not looking for a narrative, or explanation, or a fixity, a prior ground: it is the waves of the groundwork that fascinate him, and the waves pass from liquid and light into the language of his representing. Here is how Valéry describes the thought of the depths of the sea:

Plains rolling or flat, forest, volcanoes, barren canyons, coral churches that wave half-living arms, phosphoric hordes, bushes of feelers, creatures in spirals, clouds of scales. . . All these imaginable but impenetrable landscapes are much haunted by the mind. We flap in our goggle helmets through colored shadows thrown by liquid skies through which sometimes, bad angels of that heaven, fly the prompt heavy forms of cruising sharks . . . (II, 253)

Valéry has a way of entering while *estranging* the medium; if a bird flies off he can't help thinking "with him he bears the center of a world and ferries it off to be set down elsewhere." Nothing he sees can stay in itself: after all, the root of metaphor, like the root of ferryboat, is "carry-over." Writes Valéry, "The whole dog is in its gaze. He throws himself at me with the same devoted leap of his eyes as of his body. He is undivided" (II, 80).

Nor is the human eye exempt from its own scrutiny:

Rapid, vagrant, irresponsible, irrepressible headquarters of vision, so many times swifter and more sentient than the body, than the very head even; drawn, driven, dodging, and settling like a fly; glutton of objects, winkler-out of ways, coupler of things apart; more volatile member of the less volatile frame, now in thrall to every distraction, now inward fixed communing with the being: it chases over the world, lost sometimes in an object only to find itself once more in darting away . . . (II, 36)

It finds itself, we do well to repeat, in darting away from itself. In this regard, the eye is the figure of the figurer: what thinks is half what it thinks about, never entirely *turned to* what it sees, but never entirely not. Take for example the following, breathtaking piece, spun forth from an item of ocular fact:

The color of a thing is that one which, out of all colors, the thing repels and cannot assimilate. High heaven refuses blue, returning azure to the retina. All summer long the leaves hold *in* the red. Charcoal gobbles everything.

To our senses things offer only their rejections. We know them by their refuse. Perfume is what the flowers throw away.

Perhaps we can only know other people by what they eliminate, by what their substance will not accept. If you are good, it is because you retain your evil. If you blaze, hurling off sparkles and lightnings, then your sorrow, gloom and stupidity are keeping house inside you. They are more you, more yours, than your brilliance. Your genius is everything you are not . . . (II, 76–77)

"I do not know what is my own," writes Valéry, "I am not even sure of this smile, nor its consequence which is half thought . . . Whatever makes me unique is mixed with the vast body and passing plenty of this place: over there, *people*, the grist of politics, *flow among a few persons*, and across my reflections a flame of air and men, endlessly reproducing itself, blows, wavers, anticipates and sometimes precisely constitutes my thought . . ." [my italics]. This is a looking somewhat alien to an American temperament, which sentimentalizes the story of the individual, and suspects the coolness of a surmounting thought.

But it is this thought—this sensual, spiritual, physical, metaphysical, metamorphical fluid-fire of thinking—that makes Valéry the astonishing writer he is in *Teste* and *Poems in the Rough* and passages from his *Dialogues*. He himself is the audience implicated in the act:

One stretch of coast is dark and clear; another indecisively crumbled and melted into the wet material of vision . . . All I see depicts the waverings of spirit as it is invaded, then deserted, by the light and shade of ideas (II, 171)

He resembles Wallace Stevens in that the feel of generality in his work, which is the feel of the motions of intellect, does not arise out of any absence of particulars: particulars are lovingly recorded everywhere. In Valéry, the impression of generality arises out of his motion *across* particulars, his freeing their relations from constraints of habit, propriety, prejudice, foreknowledge. His discipline stands as a salutary counter-example to our narrative habit of using the predictable to fill in what isn't visible. Valéry is like the Picasso in Gertrude Stein's declaration that "Most of the time we see only a portion of the person with us, the other parts are hidden by a hat or clothes or by light or shadow. Every one is accustomed to completing the whole entirely by memory. But when Picasso saw a single eye, the other ceased to exist for him." And so with Valéry: each is all, there is no MISSING wholeness.

> Everything that is mental, thought itself makes me think of a witch's stew in a pot. It simmers, it bubbles, it foams and sings—making combinations, dissociations, precipitates. There's a bit of *everything*. That's it—everything!
>
> I have tried (as if I were not *in* one after another of these soups) to conceive that All is in this pot, a pot we never think of. All is simply one *property of a pot*, a vessel, a receptacle, a container. To say *all* is to form an enclosure, an envelope; and then to locate something outside it—which is to say that *All is not all!* . . . Shall I put God in this pot, or is He *all* that is outside it? . . . "Consciousness of self" seems to be the sensation of the mixture's striking against the pot's wall . . .
> (VI, 143)

What Lyotard writes about the painter Adami could as well be said of Valéry: "There can be no work of art if the seer and the seen do not hold one another in an embrace, if the immanence of the one for the other is not manifested and glorified, if the visual organization doesn't make us feel that our gaze has been seen and that the object is watching."[17] (This is, of course, the whole thrust of Rilke's "Archaic Torso of Apollo.")

If you think you know yourself, you haven't looked far enough—into that distance where your strangeness is. You hold more than you know, and that's how knowing *opens*. Emilie Teste remarks about her husband, Monsieur Teste (a remark that could do honor to Paul Valéry himself, for it is a reader's tribute, catching perfectly the paradox of mutually inextricable sense and contents, seer and seen): "I love his eyes. They are a little larger than visible things." It is the kind of looking Valéry described as "the stranger's way of looking at things, the eye of a man who does not recognize . . . it belongs to the thinker. It is also the eye of a dying man, a man losing recognition. In this, the thinker is a dying man" (VI, 79).

In an America that frequently seems more concerned with the permissible than the perceptible, more intent on covering and recovering than on discovering, the remark seems prophetic, the forecast looks dim. The watchman talks to himself; as for the others, they have their Walk-men on . . . What solitudes, what failures to respond or understand, what islandings . . .

But still, I insist, on some of the islands there are Crusoes. And in the imaginations of some of these solitary Crusoes crop up possibilities again, othernesses lived precisely for their difference, in flourishes of insight, wonderments of words. Let Valéry recall his audience. Let Valéry invent us, Valéry who cannot close except to open up, flourishing the very sign and stylus of all *écriture*:

Although he was alone on his island, he wore a plume in his hat—it seemed to him that by doing this he created someone to look at the plume. (II, 314)

Broken, As in English

What We Make of Fragments

"... by what language other than fragmentary—other than the
language of shattering, of infinite dispersal—can time be marked ... ?"
—Maurice Blanchot, *The Writing of the Disaster*

*

The fragment is a form we approach in aftermath (its alternative status, as the product of forethought, is rarer, and sponsors a special set of reflections, some of which I'll come to later). The study of fragments is the study of time's effects, and an artifact's endurances. Poets establish what remains, sang Hölderlin, himself the poet of the fragmentary, and what remains in time are fragments, traces, debris. Nothing lasts longer than ruins, Brodsky remarked. And time reduces works to patterns of extent and extinction; yields up fortunes of was, not will.

Still, the fact of fragmentation creates the possibility of the fragmentable: and this is the mind's art, the art of apprehension and precaution (for the mind can make time, for a time, seem small).

The writer around whom the rummaging or rubbling of deterioration goes on represents *us to* something, rather than representing something to us. For just as the act changes in time, the reader changes in the act (you never read the same book twice). What we mean at the moment we write and what we mean at the moment we *are read* are both bifold (transitive and in-); so literary meaning starts fourfold and goes from there, split on split. In a charged field, difference makes things spin.

This essay is itself a piece in pieces: my own energies tend toward centrifugal spray rather than tidy consolidation. My sources are wildly various: they range from tatters of Archilochus (recovered from German mummy-windings) to Tom Phillips's book-breakage. Friedrich Schlegel (dean of the Romantic fragmentists) took pains to distinguish the fragment of intent from that of mere extent: "Many works of the ancients have *become* fragments; many works of the moderns *begin* that way."[18] But in- or ex-, it is the *tending* of text I am interested in. I turn by nature toward the patterns of accident, the accident of patterns. We mean one way, and then another: mean *to*, then wind up, quite intransitive, meaning otherwise.

The composings of the Atheneum group (Schlegel et al.) were written not to be, but to have been, broken: their fragments were intended as small wholes, as apothegms or epigrams. And though the authorial intent was to shift prose from the explicative toward the implicative, these pieces are in fact tendentious, as a whole: they direct the reader; they have direction's end in mind. "One should drill," says Schlegel, "where the board is thickest."[19]

The point of drilling the hole in the thickest part is to *intend* the hole: is to protect its shape. And from what? The ravages of time's hole-making, which works where the material's thinnest. The hole *intended* is protected from the hole *extended* (mind against time, which threatens all our groundworks—whether of wood, or stone, or ideology).

What we have of many Greek poets is what was left after the epochs of accident passed them on to us—papyruses partly rotted, stoneworks broken.[20] We try to reconstruct their shape, but now around the work of an unintending shapemaker (time betraying itself in patterns not chaotic). Behind the excerpting done by time, there remains the idea of the original, itself from the outset a piece of something. A look at Heraclitus is a look at a collection of nuggets, for he writes, as far as we can tell even on reconstruction, in bon mots or witticisms. These were preserved by later commentators and by the memories of his listeners, and their records then were eaten away by age before we got them. The hallmark of the joke or witticism everywhere is its capacity to be remembered and repeated; a certain combination of portability, packedness and persistence is characteristic, even requisite. The Heraclitus his preservers have passed on to us is a wag: a kind of pre-Socratic stand-up comic, surviving in quick jabs, polished gems, one-liners. This kind of fragment beats time to time's prerogative: even after the papyrus falls apart, the pieces seem unbroken. This is aphorism's gift, or present.

By contrast the fragments of Archilochus and Empedocles seem not so much rearticulated as disarticulated: their missing parts (like Dickinson's dashes) are indispensable connectors. Instead of intact one-liners, we get one-phrasers and one-worders: such pieces as "curled wool," "tender horn," "sparks in wheat," and "touched girl" bob in the flow of the collected Archilochus like bits of flotsam, cork or quirk, from a once-coherent world now blasted into bits. Of the cosmogonies of Empedocles and Parmenides, their senses of how the world was put together, time has given us only a sundered version, parts and atoms twisted out of time (in the "now" of the now-ravaged text, time tends to twist itself). And so we have the world as if undone—a reminder of the two kinds of undoneness, that of parts before assembly and that of parts after disassembly, before creation or after apocalypse. So of their cosmogonies we get scraps of raw material: "copper mixed with tin," "hair, leaves, thick birdfeathers, scales," "a bell, a bough of flesh."

Sometimes a right-hand margin has fallen away, and left a left (scholars in such situations must mount peculiar salvage operations). The text is produced not only, then, by the archaic writer himself (the originator), but also by what Hugh Kenner calls "co-author Chronos," and by scholars, translators, and the reader herself, whose horizon can extend (or not) to the occasions of the given text. The Archilochean fragments I've cited can, to my mind, suggest the overall colors of an Archilochean temper. This entity I'm calling Archilochus is my postulated author, a man consistent with the contents of the peculiar whole of his surviving works (the two hundred and ninety fragments we call, in a moment of inadvertent hilarity, his "complete fragments"). Even these four scraps ("curled wool," "tender horn," "sparks in wheat," and "touched girl") seem in themselves to comprise a character: the sensual, sexual, fabulous, and profane poet we ascribe the oeuvre to. In a sense, he *is* the narrative we ascribe to them, even more than he is the narrator who inscribed them.

We can't help, as readers (or as spectators, for that matter—the science of moving pictures was predicated on this fact) putting together the separate frames into a coherent or continuous experience. For the mind is not only analytic but synthetic. The peculiar convergence of these functions is the point of an enterprise like that of the contemporary British artist Tom Phillips, whose revision of a tendentious nineteenth-century novel (*A Human Document*, by W. H. Mallock) was a parody of the very ravages and ruination Mallock's Romantic era sentimentalized. A look at some of the texts will show you to what extent Phillips is playing with the whole historic range, starting from classical fragments. Using the fatality and accidents of print, the happenstance of where things fall on the page of the original text, Phillips's lyric economies and deft reflexiveness subvert Mallock's meaning but employ Mallock's own text to do so—that is, judiciously selected portions of it. In undermining he underlines (by

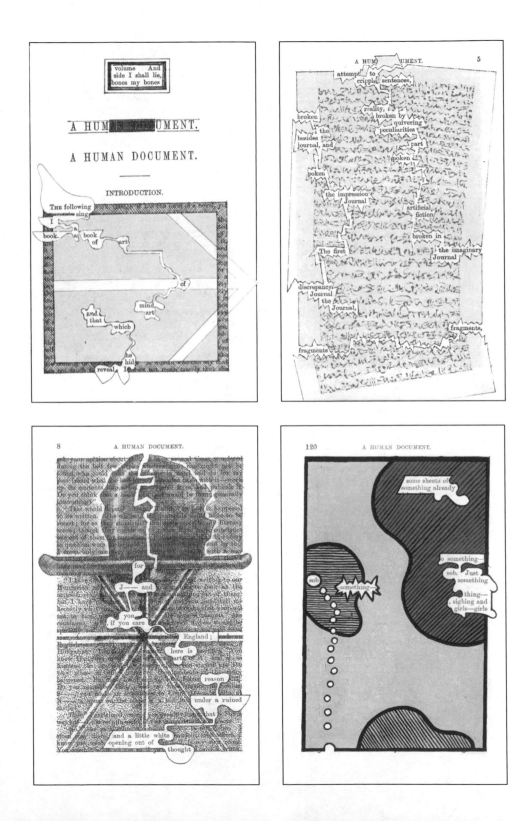

"And what sort of childhood was it?"

to say.
enough to say
to say—
loneliness
the word
going
at the same time
in the sky
organ sounded.
the sea
struck me suddenly
whisper
be good to me
whisper
often
the glass
moved
about the meaning of the petals,

the movements of a young girl's thoughts

The whole history of it is so vague.

I can't quite tell.

hardly books

it was

eagerly, gradually
the words that I heard
I put these aside as
an opera
an insufficient one;
still organ
for what—
me,
me,

the libretto of the music, of the music

—I can't tell

I can't tell

but all was for the same thing
to capture in drawing, and to express in music,
thought and study,

the loss,

the least important

moon
I myself am

myself

in search of an object for love?
way?' Yes and no—
enter
myself
associating
me,
and
me. It made me
within me some mystery.

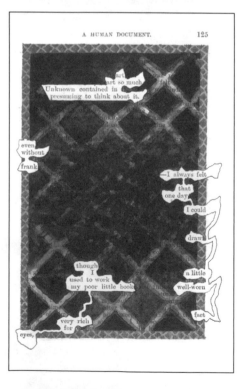

art
art so much felt
Unknown contained in presuming to think about it.

even without frank

I always felt
that
one day
I could

draw

though I used to work my poor little book

a little
well-worn
fact

very rich for
eyes,

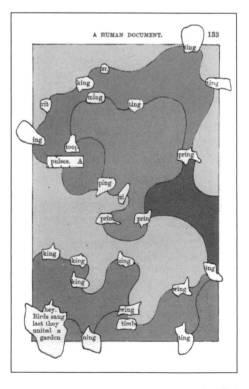

ting
zi.
king
ming
ting
rit
ing
toop
pring
pulses. A
ping
zi
prin
prin
king
king
zing
icing
ing
hey.
Birds sang last they united a garden
wing
wing
timb
ping
ting

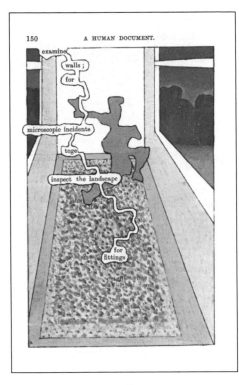

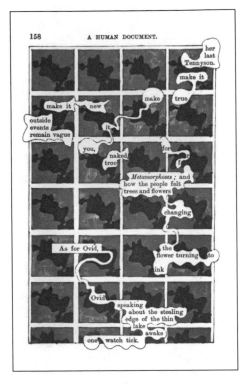

I dream with my pen balanced in my hand, fragments of poetry —fragments

like a rose is boast is boast

I drew so many words,

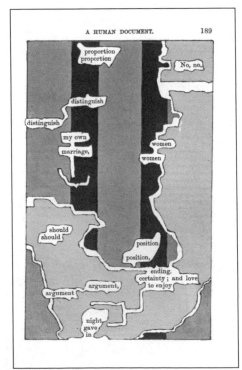

I myself am made of

I—I,

Do I mean them

I do.

dawn

early

struck

came drifting in

Amongst the dim figures that emerged and hastened looked at him

a man—

religio

anda

arel

erless gree

ajol

orro orro

orbi

ordina

methin

sidera iffer

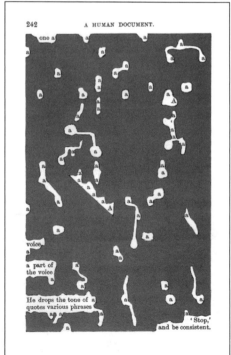

one a

voice

a part of
the voice

He drops the tone of a
quotes various phrases

'Stop,'
and be consistent.

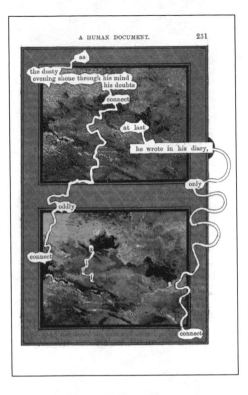

as
the dusty
evening shone through his mind
his doubts
connect
at last
he wrote in his diary,
only
oddly
connect
connect

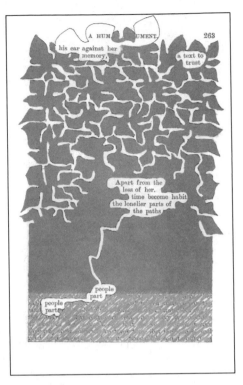

his ear against her
memory,
a text to
trust
Apart from the
less of her.
time become habit
the lonelier parts of
the paths
people
part
people
part

—I foresee it all.
in the eyes—
in the garden,
little to say.
a crumpled
last night.

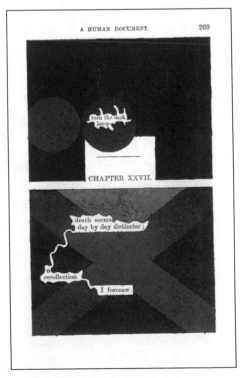

turn the dark
lamp.

CHAPTER XXVII.

death seems.
day by day distincter ;
recollection
I foresaw

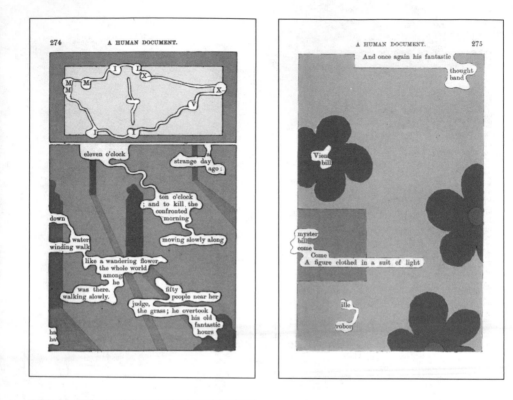
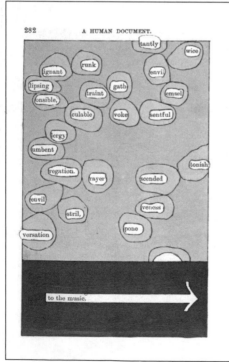
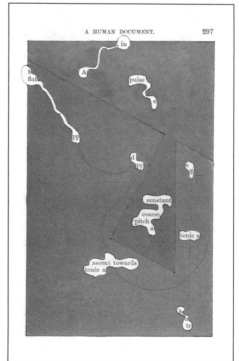

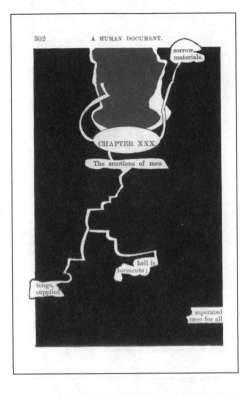

sorrow.
materials.

CHAPTER XXX.

The emotions of men

hell is
torments ;

tongs,
supplied

separated
once for all

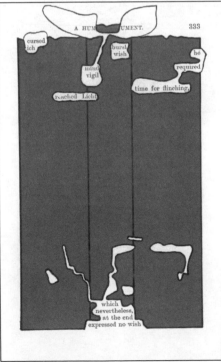

cursed
ich

burst
wish

he

mind
vigil

required

reached Licht

time for flinching,

which
nevertheless,
at the end
expressed no wish

not in lead or wood,
give the earth to me,

—the test of how
I see things now

a pavilion
for hours,

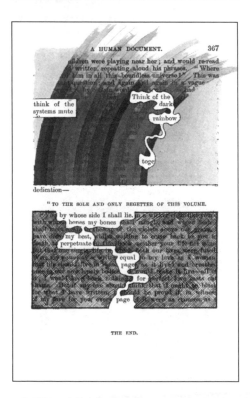

children were playing near her; and would re-read
written, repeating aloud his phrases. "Where
him in all this boundless universe?" This was
question; and again and again in a vague
had

think of the
systems mute

Think of the
dark

rainbow

toge

dedication—

"TO THE SOLE AND ONLY BEGETTER OF THIS VOLUME.

by whose side I shall lie.
bones my bones
have done my best,
perpetuate
equal
page
for
page

THE END.

omission as often as by remission) the political and literary dispositions of the original; he alludes to the Romantic operation while performing a deconstructive one. In the texts that follow, read to notice the play of (p)arts and (w)holes; catch the music and graphics of textile administration; study the ways an isolation emphasizes and a repetition differs.

*

Phillips has used the 1892 novel as his physical and philosophical ground, creating a second work by editing, obliterating, painting around and over, collaging, renegotiating, and highlighting details on the pages of the original text. The whole question of originality is a complex one, as it arises here: to do his work, Phillips uses actual copies of the original edition of the novel. The "original" texts are already replications by publication; but Phillips takes their physicality as his starting-point, and then his own version of the book (now regrounded or unearthed as *A Humument* by Tom Phillips) is published in London almost a hundred years later. The process amounts to an extraordinary critique, subversion, hijacking (or underjilling) of a text.

Phillips's book-making enterprise is repeatedly, throughout the 368 pages, made the book's own subject. Almost all the pages reprinted here amount to *ars poeticas* of one kind or another. See for example his page 150, where stanza is made a room, again, in etymological faith; and where the construction is made the site of incident, the landscape the site of the joinery; one senses an allusion to the literalizing of representation that went on at the edges of the modern, in Escher and Magritte. The framing of the enterprise itself is close to Phillips's heart (the framing of the heart itself is close to Phillips's mind). These pieces remind us of the instability of our grounds at the boundaries of such oppositions as the factitious and the natural, the novel and the autobiography, the original and the replicated, the self and the other, written and read, broken and whole.

Not the least of wonders in this "treated" novel is its capaciousness (for all its brokenness)—its range of hints, rents, laughs, leaps, riffs and references, through Latin, German, Italian, French and English, through art, poetry, music, philosophy, history, critical theory, over fences between fields and into (instead of out of) the pen—itself transgressor and transgressed—of the animal.

The relationship between his text (riven on the page by his own art as reviser/ravager) and the archaic texts befalling us in fragments of papyrus or marble isn't unremarked by Phillips (see his pages 5, 158, 237, 274, 275). Indeed, he's consciously invoking such tabulary antecedents as the

Rosetta Stone (p. 202) and Mosaic tablets, Genesis letters-of-law: for in that beginning, too, was (Somebody Else's) word.

The breaking up of monolithic logos, the gulfs and fissuring, the cracks and separations in the material of an ideality come to be the defining features of Phillips's work. They come, over time, to mark not only the break-ups of lovers, the chasms of feeling between people in twos and companies, but also those within divided selves, as multiples merge or singlenesses split. The site of these markings is the overflowing or the sub-divided page, with lines of separation that function as graphic allusions to classical columns and cartoon frames alike, speech balloons coming loose from their humans, chapter numbers turning into Roman-numeral clocks, time cropped and crooned, abbreviated and extended, rocked and rued. There are frames within frames, books within books; there are win-dows and spectacles of relativistic vantage; there are museum settings and comic-book soma-sonic pow-wows; there are lines *of* words broken by lines *between* words, vertical spaces become connected fissures. In the act of meditating on his containment by the Mallock structure, and our social and literary containments in convention (not to mention temporal con-tainments in eventuality), between the axes of the horizontal sentence and the sentence of the vertical phallus (for which Stein's counterpart is the booked box, female), Phillips does virtuosic geometries of re-enactment and escape, training our eyes on the accidents of passage, page, and juxta-position. On any Mallock page he can find multiplied singletons to isolate (194, 242), or couplings to expose (189); the double-influx is usually a sign of lovemaking, coming to some delta or puddle (if not of concomi-tance, then at least of consanguinity).

The love story that unfolds in these pages is tormented: it's all ups and downs, and the hero's name (Toge) can be taken, compositionally speaking, only from the words "together" or "altogether" (to-get-her is the hero's raison d'être). The protagonist's name is, thus, always already broken English.

With Phillips, acts of art are already editorial acts. We select as soon as we say or see. The holes seem as powerful as the fillings: page 5's crippled sentences and broken journal are all written between the lines of the torn page; the spoken (pointed) has fallen silent, into the poken (torn), the whole into the hole. This early page is one of a number that act as works of self-presentation or *ars poetica*. One of the paradoxes of containment and escape always present for us as speaking beings is the paradox of a self-representation: the self divided from the start. The hat the poem's presentation wears on page 8 is two hats, for a mind that doesn't want to be made up. The self-references on page 120 are emblemmatic: there's the palette of the painter, and the viol of the musician, and the finger-holes are holes in the very material that frames the Roy-Lichtensteinian page (a lot of *Licht*s will happen later, when the lights and darks of death begin developing toward the end of the book); the fingerholes are paint-holes, punctures, precipitating down from eyehole (tears in a peace of mind). The language seeming literally to fall, into sobs and somethings, then to burst into curvers (girls), is the language of contemporaneity. Yet a short two pages later the frame of the seen is based on older conven-tions—a *recherche du temps perdu*, with all the lyricism of those premises conveyed in its poetry, "about the meaning of petals, the movements of a young girl" (here the meaning of "about" moves from one sense to another, from meaning toward movement). These two pages (120 and 122) are part of a retrospective streak in the middle of the book, jour-nal as personal history. In the public book-format is encoded the private: what-happened-to-me becoming indistinguishable from what-happened-to-be. The whole elaborate concentricity of Phillips's enterprise relies on rich senses of time: the readers we are have to recognize the reader he is (both of Mallock and himself, both of present self and of past ones, as on p. 124). The daily fluctuations of pride and humiliation, avidity and despair, ravenousness and resignation are recorded, page by page, as the book progresses (does a book progress as time progresses? yes and no). The effect of mind merging with and diverging from itself makes even single voices seem to be engaging in interior conversation: on page 242, for example, the very sign of singularity, the article a, is multiplied from one to two to four to more, until the writer, having made his point musi-cally as well as grammatically indefinitely extensible, cuts himself short with a rebuke. The range of tones and temperaments (such characteriza-tions are psychological as well as musical) is virtuosic.

The twelve selves of page 202 are (h)ours, striking the artist in the act of his self-remarking. The administered tonics of page 297 have en-coded dynamic markings, and end in a trill. A score and more. The music made by birds on page 133 is present-participial, and the *rit* is a *ritar-dando*, marking a slowing tempo in Italian; but it's also a third-person laugh, in French, and a homonym for the writers' own object, writ, a participle complex that can make noun flow, verb fix. The image Phillips inscribes these sound-pulses *into* is the garden with its Adam and Eve ten-ants, containing a tree and the earth it's bending toward. The previous page boasted a similar climax-turned-to-a-fall, with its passage from high and sunny innocence (the "diary of a child") downward in time and space to a low point, where marriage is added to Mr. Glad (at the lowest hole in the human figure, counterpart in color and form to the head-hole above). Love can't seem to be made for good.

The sorrow is the writer's as well as the lover's. (P. 302 reads "Sorrow materials. The emotions of men. Tongs supplied. Hell is torments. Separated once for all.") For the writer's wish to arrive would mean to satisfy and thus annihilate the desire that drives him. See page 333, and then, on page 353, "the first stone cast / against names / Words—words! / Make me / a rose," where the outcry is across the gulf between desire and incarnation, not only in the lover but in language too. Page 159, remember, gave us "a rose / is / a / boast / is / a / boast / . . .": like Stein, Phillips knows predication is an unstable ground, and he can't find a resting-place in saying "is"; can't find a resting-place in being. His own self-consciousness keeps breaking up the unity he yearns for. The book is about the bookmaker's walking THAT line. "People part" (263) is itself a fragment and a whole, depending how you read it, depending whether "part" is noun or verb. The art's *in* parts, as Toge is in the altogether.

So we find "broken syllables which / are for lovers signs" (235); and "broken again / the lot he had chosen / studying sudden" (260); and "a text to trust / Apart from the / less of her" (262); and, finally, homing to his own art's sensuality, a text of broken language, arriving at a sign: "to the music," its arrow pointing off-page (282).

These scraps of text, highlighting language arts as graphic and as musical fields, wind up in a kind of cosmogony too ("think of the dark rainbow" comes last—no light promises!—and then the final rededication of the book at the end, itself recalling the concentricity of debts, to lovers and writers who came before, and lover and readers who come after). Page 366, the next to last, begins with an Empedoclean kind of constituent: "not in lead or wood, / give the earth to me," and ends "a pavilion / for hours." The earth of lead and wood is natural earth; but a box of lead and wood is a coffin; and the making of things with lead and wood could be the making of a pencil. What is creation made of, and what do we make of it? Such questions ground Phillips's fragmenting art, just as they were the gist of Parmenides's fragmented one.

Page 196 offers us only two phrases but the two suffice to suggest the whole complexity of Phillips's engagement with human histories as histories of fragment: one is the phrase "bound Toge." Toge is tied to the word he's taken from; he's broken from it, too. And "bound" itself, as a pun, suggests both the immobilized (tied-up) and moving (for bound as verb can break out of its stiller moment, and one of the meanings of bound as an adjective is destined). In these second senses (in which Toge is bound to-get-her again) Toge is bound for, rather than bound by. He is headed somewhere.

The human head is, of course, the place where such double-binds make their home, and where the second phrase ("Keep enough future") aims its inventory-advice. "Enough future" is what Phillips saves of Mallock. It is a kind of rueful *carpe diem*, extending its peculiar temperament and temporality across the usual bounds. For will works in the present, and the English store of time has three communicating rooms. The future, where we've always tended to put eternity, is here susceptible of quantification: just enough endlessness! Making a circle from the first to the last dedication, besetting to begetting, work to love, *A Humument* binds self to other, sameness to difference, time to time. If a future can be *kept*, it's already here. In which direction are we headed? One in which we can look forward to the past?

Page 269's dark testimony ("death seems / day by day distincter") is accompanied by a brightening paradox: "a / recollection / I foresaw." This might be the book's best *ars poetica*: in time, the book's space is a hinge, a *brisure*, a breaking place, a joining place. The book is a monument to pieces, a monument of pieces, a monument in pieces.[21]

*

All poetry is fragment: it is shaped by its breakages, at every turn. It is the very art of turnings, toward the white frame of the page, toward the unsung, toward the vacancy made visible, that wordlessness in which our words are couched. Its lines insistently defy their own medium by averting themselves from the space available, affording the absent its say, not only at the poem's outset and end but at each line's outset and end. Richard Howard's deft maxim ("prose proceeds, verse reverses") catches the shifts in directionality implicit in the advertencies of verse. It means to aim at (as its means are) the untoward.

A composed verse is a record of the meeting of the line and sentence, the advertent and the inadvertent: a succession of good turns done. The poem is not only a piece, like other pieces of art; it is a piece full of pieces. Schlegel says, in poetry every whole can be a part and every part really a whole. The line from Parmenides that contains the whole of the Parmenidean enterprise is: "You can't say nothing." But the saying so, itself, is framed by the nothing, is wrested from it. Reading the pre-Socratics I was struck by what seemed uncannily frequent references to the very ravages of time and accident that were indeed going to cut the poetic materials to shreds.

This irony arises most conspicuously in the fragments of Archilochus, which float on the page in the Davenport edition in pools and swells of empty space, seeming themselves a pointed commentary on the absences abutting them.

> [   ]
>   He replied.

Or, to take another:

> Utterly unrefined

(this one is a fragment one can't help reading in light of its own fragmenthood: utterly *rede*fined by time and decay)

>   one half,
> one third

(Here too a contemporary reader can hardly fail to consider the fact of fragmenthood itself)

> [   ]
>   from what
> [   ]

(Almost hilariously illustrating our readerly concern with origin and intention, source and destination, this fragment stands as a sign of such missing frames. Whatever words the writer might have placed

> where now the archaeologizer's
> brackets survive, one finds oneself
> all the more deeply moved by their
> absence, and by the prominence
> assumed by words ("from what")
> which elsewise might have seemed
> relatively insignificant)

Given other fragments as abbreviated as "(wa)x-soft" and "n" (!), one can't help being uneasy at the presumptions of "translation": half the scholarship on the pre-Socratics consists in conjecture about the missing portions. (The critical community having been given so powerful a hermeneutic postrogative, a reader sometimes feels inclined to come to the silent author's defense by adding to fragment 157 ("he turned") three more words in his behalf ("in his grave").

My own ignorance of Greek and forgetfulness of Latin make me rely on the translations I happen to have at hand. This is a further accidentality, I know, which I call down upon my enterprise. But I am not merely resigned to accident: I am committed to it. I accept the risks involved; that is, I treat these pieces as if they had been written in English. I see such recourse only partly as a risk—also sometimes it proposes opportunities, and in some senses it is always the inescapable ground of knowing (we are always translating from the evidence of our senses, which may be fatally circumscribed from the start.) As Allen Grossman reminds us in his feast of fragments, *Summa Lyrica*, "The stone is of more kinds than the inscription." But the gone (in all the ways we conjure up what *isn't*) is of more kinds than the stone. And with already fragmented texts, we can't help doing reconstructive acts of reading, no matter *how* Greek Greek is to us.

*

Where the right-hand margin of Archilochus was ripped away, we are left with the left:

Desire,
Future,
Enemy.
Music:
My song
And a flute
Together

(Here the vertical became, itself, a temporal feature, and the poem a piece scored for text and time.)

And here is a right-hand margin, from another torn page (fragment 154):

> moves against;
> staunching,
> sharp pointed penis,
> I, as usual,
> situate;
> suffice.
> the city,
> therefore you imagine,
> we establish beauty.

Among the pleasures of such accidents is their occasional matchability: the two margins almost fit each other, and the poem that results seems characteristically Archilochean:

> Desire / moves against
> Future, / staunching
> Enemy. / Sharp pointed penis,
> Music: / I, as usual
>   / situate;
>   / suffice.
> My song / the city,
> And a flute . . . / therefore you imagine
> Together / we establish beauty.

The poem's last lines seem attributable to the binding-together itself: the mind tends to bind the floating pieces, as is the mind's wont, in the face of incompletion and brokenness.

Empedocles seems almost to have foreseen the "diasporaction" (McFarland's term) of the text, its vulnerability to (or enrichment at) the hands of the world to come. Fragments such as 88 ("one vision generated by two eyes") and "one joint binds two things," and "no part of the Whole is empty or full," and "better to say twice what needs to be said"— all seem to move from authored event toward readerly eventuality. Again and again one gets the hint of a metafragmental commentary within the original Empedoclean text: the single word "uncreated," for example, seems much broader in its solitude than it may have been, attached to any noun; suggestive too are lines like " 'originate' is only a word," and "only fools incapable of connected thought / believe that anything that Is can pass into nothingness"; and "look with your mind, don't sit dazed by vision"; and "and if no emptiness, no room for addition."

Paradoxes of wholeness and completeness prompt a readerly question, concerning Empedocles's fragments 18 ("love") and 19 ("tenacious love"), which is the greater love. For though the ordinary assumption is that the tenacious is the greater, still a qualified noun is a restricted one, and tenacious no less than transient love is love that is modified, a subset of the larger category. Even tenacious love is not unbounded, overlooking as it may the charms of the passing, or the uncontainabilities of the fleeting . . . Archilochus was more evidently an ironist (a professional attribute, perhaps, since he claims both the warrior and the lover roles at once). Indeed, one feels the both-at-onceness of his trades when he wishes "to engage with an insatiable girl, / Ramming belly against belly, / Thigh riding against thigh." In the fragment that gives us "jeopardy on two horns," is it we who bring to the reading the sense of its author's perennial dilemma, caught between horns of love and war, between time and translation, between holes and hard places? Or we who, given only the fragment "lips covered in foam," sense extremities both of battlefield and bed? It may be his own spicing as much as time's splicing that makes Archilochus so alive for us. Even in these ravaged texts he seems a fully human presence, his follies confessed ("feet were of the highest value there"), his ironies sharpened ("they fled, seven of them fell, and each of all our thousand claimed their kill"), his appetites pointed ("there's risen bread in my spear, / wine in my spear, / and when I drink I couch with my spear"). In its portrait of Archilochus, time has preserved such snippets as "damp crotch," "elegant frog," "biting sword," "eaten by fleas," and whole sassy sentences like "my prong's unreliable / and has just about / stood his last." Contextual flavor amounts to portraiture. And so when we get so slender a fragment as "how? up from beneath?", we bring from our constructive labors a coherer's sense of the man, to supply a wealth of simultaneous readings: it's about military strategy and sexual strategy; it's about time's indirection; it's about the grounding of the text . . .

In the following Archilochus piece, its Alexandrian page variously torn (torn left side, right side, top and bottom, and with moth-holes in the middle, adds Davenport with diabolical exactitude) I can't help finding a delicate and deeply suggestive poem, with all the insinuation of a William Carlos Williams (or a Beckett) piece:

> You
>   if
> river
>   so
> around
> I, then, alone

A reader readied by practice with broken texts will find sweet patterns here, of line and circle, current and recurrency, a lover's count-down from second to first and finally, in time, the missing person . . . The first five words resisting lineation seem to float, as if by virtue of the river, or the one who rives (for in the absence of a verb in either territory, the you's five lines or the I's one, "river" starts to look sinuously verb-like); at last a true and horizontal line seems to form, but in it the first person finds itself stranded rather than connected: commas separate its parts. And isn't this also the fragment's account of its own fragmenthood, given the arrows and circles of time? If and then, around and alone, the hints fall into patterns. But it was time that gave us the chance to read these sad shreds so.

*

You must expect the unexpected, says Heraclitus, or you won't get it. Though Heraclitus was dubbed "the obscure" by ancient writers, in fact his paradoxes seem transparent, luminous. There is a reason "no one steps twice into the same river" lasted so long: it is so economical and so rich with suggestion about sameness and time (not only is the river never the same, but one*self* isn't the same; so in addition to the question about sameness are raised questions about one-ness, about ness-ness). "People do not understand how, while differing from itself a thing can be in agreement with itself—a backturning connection, like that of a bow or a lyre," says Heraclitus. Here is an *ars poetica* for poets, if ever there was one. Like a bow or lyre!—what kills or calls, what causes curves and curves a cause. The thing *turns on* itself; this is virtually verse's etymology. There are plenty of puns in Heraclitus, I am told; and one of them is *bios*: depending where you place the stress, it is bow or life. Either way, he's saying, its job is to kill.

The work of Heraclitus, as we inherit it, seems despite its sunderings to have been fashioned for a fullness. He has already cut his gems and polished up their facets: each saying seems ready to stand alone, to carry its weight. All animals are driven to the pasture with a blow, he says, and knows his readers know the word for pasture is the word for law, with just a difference of stress. It is still the same road, he says elsewhere, going up or down. The sun is one foot wide, he writes. This wisdom has the bite of wit as surely as the agenbite of inwit, for "the sun is one foot wide" may mean we're large, or it is small; it may mean man's the measure of all things, or man is sunk in false and self-obsessed perspectives.

This wit of the pre-Socratics shows up best in their aphoristic moments: Archilochus said "the fox knows many things, but the hedgehog knows one big thing"; and, "what breaks me, young man, is tasteless desire, dead iambics, boring dinners" (how cleverly in this latter declaration he reworks the more predictable series, boring iambics, dead desire, and tasteless dinners!) Heraclitus wittily observes, "If the sun didn't exist, it would be night all day long." And he passes on a story about Homer, urging us to notice the unapparent: the kids ask Homer a riddle: "If we find it and catch it, then we leave it here; but if we can't find it, then we take it with us." The answer is something you can get without knowing it: lice. Than Heraclitus no one but Archilochus has more pointed a sense of humor: "Doctors," says Archilochus, "cut up and burn and variously torment their patients and then complain they are not paid enough." And similarly, somewhat closer to a poet's heart (since a poet is not a critic, and the root of criticism is *krinein*, to cut): "The way of writing's straight and crooked." Like Heraclitus, he surprises us by making, in a quick sally of redirection, something feeling whole.

It is quite another matter to read a writer like Parmenides, whose wisdoms lead us *past* the gates of light, toward darker grounds, ones that can't be rationally rounded out or wholly comprehended. With Parmenidean incompletion, one feels the Keatsian credential at work, the negative capability that keeps a poet from reaching too impatiently and quickly for what's known or explicable. Whereas Heraclitus and Archilochus make us feel amazed at how much we can know despite the fragmenting, Parmenides reminds us how little we know even with unbroken evidences. He reminds us, in short, how inherently broken knowing is.

When we read these writers we always feel a poignant effect of the time differential: *our* knowing what befell them, individually, and what befell their world. This particular historical knowledge (given us by time) adds another twist to the presence of their texts. So when we read Ovid's "Let others praise ancient times, I was glad I was born in these"—we smile from altitudes of sympathy. He didn't know (we think) how utterly he'd come to embody those "ancient times" for us; but we don't know (in that same sense) to what extent we shall ourselves embody ancientness for others. Even in a human lifetime, this not-knowing plays its rue-inducing part.

But there is another not-knowing to which the writer's words serve as testimony, and that is the not-knowing we welcome and explore, the not-knowing all knowers share. The curious fragment in the Nietzsche archives, the scrap of a sentence unattached to any other text or document, its quotation marks carefully included—"I have forgotten my umbrella" —records one such not-knowing. The poignant point is his having *re-*

membered the forgetting, his having recorded the re*called* but not re*covered* thing. It is precisely too, for me, about acts of language: indicating what they can't embody. (Bodily acts suffer this same sorrow when they mean to indicate great ideas: that is why acts of love are finally so poignant; maybe this is even the source of all post-coital tristesse: for love acts mean to mean some endlessness, and yet are throbbed through with ends, with a mortal metric, with a vengeance.) And it is in this sense that acts of language too are acts of elegy.

*

Parmenides of all the ancient poets is the most alert to the problems posed by acts of language-making. It is in Parmenides that the paradoxes of thinking and speaking are most explicitly addressed, and one can't read the Parmenidean fragments without constantly being reminded of the thought-waves of a Heidegger or Wittgenstein. In short, Parmenides thinks as follows: There are two ways for thinking, and one of them is unthinkable. Being is, and has to be; or nothing is, and has to be. The second way cannot be held in mind: you cannot know what isn't, nor can you name it. Nothing cannot be said, nothing cannot be known. What's there for thinking is what's there for being. What is more, what exists cannot be discontinuous—it isn't more existent in some clumps or patches than in others, more real here than there (words make us think things clump). What is cannot be incomplete: it is not lacking, but if it were, it would lack everything. Unbeginning, it is unperishing, since it is whole and indivisible. (Out of what "other" would being come to be? he asks. There is no other we can think of; and what is there to think of, he insists, is there to be.)

One reader, Sparshott, after reading this extraordinary trail of meditations, put it this way: "Parmenides long ago said 'To be and to be thought of are one and the same.' Or did he say, 'Only what can think can exist'? Or even, 'Thinking and being are the same'? A certain crankiness in his venerable syntax, or perhaps even in his venerable character, prevents us from ever being quite sure." Sparshott notwithstanding, how glad I am for such uncertainties. That Parmenides proceeds so exactingly and arrives so cloudily is his great strength; it is as profound a paradox as that proposed by being alive at all.

Let me run a few more Parmenidean wisdoms by you, for your pleasure. Like the *Tao Te Ching* (which warns its readers "the five colors confuse the eye, / the five sounds dull the ear . . .") Parmenides reminds us to beware the aimless eye and ringing ear, and to beware of habit.

Humans make the mistake (by nature, perhaps by bilaterality) of proposing always to oppose; constructing always two and only two forms in mind, two sides bodied forth. But all is full, says Parmenides, of light and dark together. (Here he is unlike Heraclitus, who makes of strife a generative alternation between opposites, one giving birth to the other in succession, in which construction one senses the Zoroastric presence, system of struggle between light and dark.) Like Lao Tse, Parmenides sees pairs of opposites as marking every moment of identity—according to the *Tao Te Ching* "high and low determine one another, front and back give sequence . . ." Parmenides's way of putting it is this: mortals have erroneously established opposing signs apart from one another (as if there were more of a separate thing called dark when there was less of another thing called light). He insists on presence; and presence is presence of mind. Set your mind on the unseen, yes, he writes, but know there is no absence. "For the full is thought."

*

The moving (not the stopping), the score of shiftings (not the final rest of destination), the finding—at a near horizon—a sudden verticality (invert, convert, pervert, advert), these are the characteristic turns of verse. In some ways Empedocles seems a revisitation of Parmenides ("I will speak in Doubles: / At times the solitary one / grows out of the man, / at times the many out of the one. / Genesis is double and death / is double, for whatever dies," he writes. But like Heraclitus he seems to see opposites as successive, not simultaneous: "The elements are the same . . . but different . . . They predominate in turn in the turning of time." This last line is full of the poetry of pre-Socratic thought, which is too often exclusively thought of as philosophy.

For though any organism or whole is an inference proceeding from fragmentary cognition, nevertheless the inference keeps proceeding. Blake's (like Stevens's) anvil rings with that forging: "The imagination is not a state; it is Human Existence itself." Parmenides said it twenty four centuries before: that thinking and being are one.

Any fragment is, itself, a small study of the conditions of the partial and the whole. When we read the Empedoclean fragment "Cutting water from five fountains / with lasting bronze," don't we read the cut of the lasting against the fountains of the impermanent? And what five fountains seem impermanent, so much as our own senses? And what is the lasting bronze that gives shape to the fountains of phenomenal perception? Is it concept that gives percept shape? It seems to me the world of phenomena, the perceptual flow, might be cut up with bronze ideals, ideas we take for lasting, acting on perceptions we take for ephemeral. Maybe that streaming of the sensory suggests some triumph of flux over fix, despite all our ideas. Perhaps rather than passing away it surpasses: maybe it outflows what outlasts . . .

Despite their place in our maxims, guts are what rots first, or is eaten away first by predators. But the gut has the last word, literally, in Empedocles (after the millenia have eaten what they will). Fragment 153 is the final fragment in scholarly reconstructions: and that fragment is a single word, and that word is "belly" (the tenderest of buttons in the flesh turned out to be the toughest in the text).

Maybe that is survival's measure: parts and *not* the whole: the human part and parcel. Though Heraclitus says "the sun is a foot wide" (chiding or cherishing us, we cannot tell), still the foot is the poem's measure. And the measure of the soul is the logos, the law, which would be translated from Greek to Hebrew to the King James as "The Word." But a lot of learning isn't understanding, says Heraclitus; again he echoes the *Tao Te Ching*: "True wisdom is different from much learning." The world according to Heraclitus, made by no man or god, always was, is and will be an everliving fire, kindled in measures and put out in measures. Thinking, he says, is a sacred disease; and sight is deceptive. An unapparent connection is stronger than an obvious one. We are separated from what we're most continually in contact with. Most people are unaware of what they do after they wake up, just as they forget what they do while asleep. They don't even know (he goes on) what they've *heard*: they are absent while present. The god the oracle speaks for neither indicates nor conceals: he gives a sign.

In Heraclitus I keep seeing that same transtemporal reflexiveness I noted in the others: fragments seeming to have ironic bearing on their own situation in history. "While changing, it stays," in the words of one of his aphorisms. And the traces of these traces show up later in the literatures that succeed them: the Parmenidean journey to the gates of insight and the goddess's revealings there about truth and appearances, these are echoed in the Bible and in Dante. The goddess's warnings about what can't be said are audible, later, in Revelations' "I heard a voice from heaven saying 'Seal up those things which the seven thunders uttered, and write them not.'" Says Allen Grossman, "Poetry is a version of the unutterable. While the poet sings, the unutterable keeps right on talking." More is left out than can ever be put in. And God himself is unpredictable—no dicting binds him. In Jonah he changes his mind, and Jonah rebukes him for going back on his word. God's word is logos, which meant (among other things, originally) an accounting. But in Heraclitus's sense of the soul, it meant measurelessness: that is the poetic measure, that limit within which the endless can be evoked, that song in which the breaking off is constantly continued.

*

Brokenness inheres in human life, for all its stories to the contrary, about itself. From inside its own account, life always seems unfinished. We can thank Thomas McFarland for bringing together one of the best collections of comments on the subject of such partialities.[22] "I can contemplate nothing but parts," said Coleridge. "The unconditioned is complete," says Kant, but adds "the unconditioned is never to be met with in experience." The monumental unity revered by idealism—where can it be said or known to exist? What we see is no less circumscribed than what we say; "there is in experience," writes Heidegger, "a permanent incompleteness which cannot be evaded."

God brings the animals to man in Genesis, in order "to see what he would call them." God is interested in man's calling, the namer's orders. In so inquiring, God himself discovers the nature of what he's made—*after* (not before) he's made it. He discovers it *in the act*. It wasn't his *intention* that interested him most. This every artist understands.

Love is partial. There is a *fulness* to forgetfulness, a part to re*membering*, an arm and a leg to our lives. It is the price of memory; wrote Anatole France, "God knows everything, but permits himself to forget." Certainly we can't ourselves be whole. Even the mental field is made of swoops of copulation, mosaic sprays. If we look at ourselves, we look at parts, we forget more than we remember. We can't see our eyes, except in reflective surfaces, and AS reflective surfaces. One favors oneself: but one is fond, as fond is founded in the foolish.

Dike the goddess (whose name is bound up with the very origins of indication) tells Parmenides: "It is all one to me where I begin, for I shall return again." Let us end on a return, as well, and return to a conversation Benjamin Haydon overheard in 1817.

It was a conversation, he said, between "two common-looking men." He overheard it in the museum where the immensely popular Elgin marbles (which inspired a whole Romantic age) were for the first time on display. These marbles, England's public chance to see the evidences of the ancient, were enormous human figures, some without heads, some without hands or feet, and they attracted droves of viewers. The living juxtaposition of small whole moving people and immense frozen human postures must have made for some amazing moments (age on age, part on part, flesh on stone). One of Archilochus's fractal scraps is "Listen to me cuss"; it's a kind of synechdoche for the whole effect of his offering to posterity (that's us).

And so too, the words of Haydon's own two fond shlemiels have been preserved, to become two more tatters in literary history. The two unlikely immortals stand, awe-struck, slack-jawed, before the wondrous age and dimensions of the grand fracture of figures before them.

"How broken they are, a'ant they?" uttered one. "Yes," the other answered; "but how *like life*."

A Genuine Article

"... *a case can be made out for the poet giving some of his life to the use of
the words* the *and* a: *both of which are weighted with as much epos and
historical destiny as one man can perhaps resolve. Those who do not believe
this are too sure that the little words mean nothing ...*"

—Louis Zukofsky [23]

*

In the beginning was the word—not *a* word. That is, it didn't seem to
matter exactly *what* word. Or perhaps the word was one that (like the
name of God) could not be spoken. In other words, the word was (if not
mum) then maybe more like *the*, itself.

In my English-speaking childhood, I took that "the" for sacred. It had
the qualities of sacredness: both its unequivocality (the word, like the
god, brooked no other) and its paradoxicality (eventually, there were to
be three gods, as there are three tenses, and the noun articulated by a
"the" has a history: it comes again, and was foreseen; it doesn't just occur,
but re- and precurs). When "the bear comes out of the woods," he'd been
known or mentioned before; when "a bear comes out of the woods,"
it's somewhat more alarming, less expected—he has not appeared before, and the hearer *starts* a little (or a lot, depending on whether she is
learning this fact in a field or in a reading chair). Articles thus operate as
time signs: they cast their light ahead, onto their subsequent nouns, but
cast a different light upon appearance ("a bear") than upon reappearance
("the bear"). The "the" presumes something already there; it reacknowl-
edges it. But an "a" makes its noun crop up on the spot: with an "a," the
unforeseen (and, by extension, the disappearing) is articulated.

"A" marks the first in an alphabetical series, and so could, one would
think, slip from cardinal to ordinal enumeration (in some uses, for ex-

ample in headings and subheadings, it does). But "the" remains the marker of pre-eminence, extra-ordination: "He is THE editor today" means one so favored as to have been promoted almost beyond comparison, quality annihilating quantity, while "he is an editor today" bespeaks a sadder fate: he was something else before, and is likely to be something else again. The "the" is the article of exclusivity: "He is THE God" escapes the question of competition by launching one god out of numbers into the realm of the one-and-only. That marker of identity, the word "same," must take "the" for its article, never "a." An "a" is not one only; it is only one.

The "the" feels in such regards coercive; it sets up its noun as an afore-mentioned entity (and yet smacks of the unduplicated).[24] As time went by, and I entered parochial school, I came to prefer my articles indefinite. A's had their own paradoxicality: they were first in a list, best of grades, but they were also the unstable article; they marked one as one among many, and everything hung on the emphasis: 1A is primo, first of the first, an honorary the; but one a is a humble thing.

*

If we came from *the* country, we came from a broad and founding sense of land, we came from the landscape, not a nation. We came from some abiding or idealized country*side*, a kind of understanding, an under-grounding connection (like that of the mushroom discovered to root in a vast and spreading subsurface fungus from which what we call individual mushrooms crop up: in the mushroom, then, the possibility arises that the category *is* the thing; it is all one, and its individuality and its kind are one and the same; in this it resembles God).

If we came from *a* country, we came from something humankind creates (as often arbitrarily as not) along a mapline, and can wipe out in the politics of a moment. Coming from "a" country, we come from something very particular, very exposed: the "a" is of surfaces, it comes into being there and marks the threshold of appearance. The article "a" draws the very (verbal) border of a coming-into-being, because the hearer or the reader knows it marks a noun about to be called, not recalled.

If the "the" tells something about the recursive past (in which its noun existed before), and the "a" tells something about the precursive future (an unforeseenness about to befall), then a poet can administer such articles for their cursive and discursive powers, savoring the time relations they incur.

*

"A" inclines toward the unfamiliar; it is the mark of the adulterer. The etymology of adultery is to the point: unrelated to *adolescere* (which means to mature), it comes rather from ad (toward) + alter (other), and so makes the familiar spouse a sameness the adulterer turns away from, turning toward an other, an im-proper, an un-self. "The" is anchored in the known; "a" sets sail toward horizons unforeseen, undefined, unclosed. Where "the" entitles, "a" unsettles. Preachers need the's; poets need a's. "The" meets its (already made) match, "a" meets its (unmatched) maker.

*

"The," by its very nature, is famous; "a," by all that is holy, is not.

*

But was a dog the same thing as the dog? For in Watt's instructions there was no mention of a dog, but only of the dog, which could only mean that what was required was not any dog, but one particular dog, that is to say, not one dog one day, and the next another, and perhaps the next a third, no, but every day the same, every day the same poor old dog, as long as the dog lived.[25]

Here the "the" proposes a mystery, because no pre-existing dog is apparent to Watt: the "the" casts back onto a pre-sumption he can't locate. The whole meditation has a great deal in common with Beckettian treatments of god (it is revealing to go back and substitute, in the passage quoted, a "god" for every "dog"). Indeed, much of *Watt* is a meditation on the shifting forms of that authority.

One of the accessory pleasures of this passage arises from the series "not one dog one day, and the next another, and perhaps the next a third." Here Beckett's delight in arithmetic puzzles and schemes can be seen to play a part. For the parallels could be taken to suggest that the counterpart of the first phrase's "one dog" is the second phrase's "the next" (and thus the counterpart of "one day" is "another"). This sets up, instead of days in line, dogs in line. So days proceed in the more arbitrary fashion, along lines of indefinite articles, from "one day" to "another" to "a third," while dogs proceed, definite, from "one dog" to "the next" to "the next."

One might rather have expected the less misreadable, more exact, parallel construction ("not one dog one day, and another the next"). But in setting up the phrases chiasmically (so that the positions of the corresponding terms are switched) Beckett actually proposes a comic disorder of serial attachments, so that dogs become orderly at the expense of days, and the order of days seems factitious, more arbitrary, in its way, than any line of dogs. The construction also makes perfectly undecidable, rhetorical arts being what they are, which of the second set of terms refers to which of the first, and thus destabilizes any secure sense we might have had of the identities of "the same" and "the other."

Indeed, the third and fourth possibilities (all of *Watt* is shot through with permutative and combinative series) come to mind: "not one dog one day, and the next the next"; and, better yet, "not one dog one day, and another another." Here the distinction (dog from day) dissolves upon repeated designation, and we come down to a long line of self-generative others, no two dogs or days alike and yet all inhabiting the single word "another" (its article incorporated and its repetition tending toward unending distinction-in-sameness) . . .

Day and dog seem switchable, too, when Beckett goes on: "every day the same, every day the same old dog." Now the question of time (punctual or continuous) arises, because "the same" in "every day the same" can be said to modify "day" as surely as "dog," and only in the incantatory subsequence ("every day the same old dog") do days distinguish themselves (among themselves) again, against the evidence, and contrast, of unchanging dog. "As long as the dog lived" caps the trail hilariously, not only because the dog has just taken on the quality of an unchanging thing and now to that unchangingness an end is proposed, but also because the dog's identity as a day has crossed our minds, not to mention the dog's identity as a god. "As long as the dog [day/god] lived," that is, all the livelong dog/day/god, as dogged as the day is long, Watt reorders lords on leads.

The last sentence in the passage, ending item three of Watt's meditations on the question of the mysterious dog, is posed in faintly legalistic terms: "But a fortiori were several dogs the same thing as the dog?" Since by now not only days but gods seem interchangeable with dogs, the question of number (are several the same as the one?) raises not only the theological question about the person(s) of God, but also the philosophical inquiry into the experience of (and constructions upon) time: "Were several days the same thing as the day?" is not without bearing on minds inheriting as much as ours do from the Greek's several senses of time ("in my day," says the synechdochizing elder, and means "in my best years"; we lease a room for "the" day and mean for the daylight hours, but we lease it for "a" day and mean a nighttime too [in the mad mathematics of time-reference in English, a day can sometimes equal a day and a night]). Such quandaries (in which we live) aren't lost on a Samuel Beckett ("a" Samuel Beckett is *the* S.B. in readers). There aren't, a fortiori, many of him.

*

Beckett, one says in tribute, is a rare one. But one is, oneself, always the rarest, the one (from one's own perspective) constitutively unlike all others. One is the one for whom one reserves an entire personal pronoun (you, he, she, and it can, from one's own perspective, apply to many beings; but one says "I" of oneself only). One is not only cardinally, but ordinally one: the *sum* and sum, the one in whom all others live.

One is not a word (said), but the word (saying); the proper name, properly considered, seems too arbitrary to be ours; we are rather the very site of the naming of being, not so much the "I" as the "am." The article pertaining to oneself is, psychologically speaking, immediate and clear. One is much more "one and only," much more the presumed case, much more the previously existing presence, much more "the," in short, than "a." One shares this attribute with God: before one was, was nothing.

*

Before *Finnegans Wake* began (with the uncapitalized "first" "word" "riverrun") there was a missing article, we tend to think. But then when *Finnegans Wake* tries to end, it can't, because an article is left dangling, and its noun, the object of an intimated preposition, seems to be missing: "A way a lone a last a loved a long the".

This last string of words is overrun with articles—and the "the" we missed at the book's beginning seems to arrive at the end (see Jacques Aubert's nice reading of the last line's relation to the first[26]). The eleven last words bring *Finnegans Wake* to a recirculator's point of return, and thus again to the first twenty-seven words of the work ("riverrun, past Eve and Adam's, from swerve of shore to bend of bay, brings us by a commodious vicus of recirculation back to Howth Castle and Environs."). The good reader of poetry (who goes from the last line to the first words again) recognizes the circle that overcomes ends (of sentences and lines); all poets know, by nature, how such recirculation works; in this regard the *Wake* is not so novel. Its return is from death-words to Genesis, and from "Given. The keys to." (just before the novel's last line) to the kingdom of Howth at the novel's beginning. Such details suggest the care with which the circle is tended. But more amazing, to my mind, than the *fact* of such a circling is the power of this line in itself to radiate readings.

Where the indeterminacy of "riverrun" as part of speech arises out of the joining of two different words (a noun plus a verb), the uncertainty attending the syntactical units in the last phrase ("A way a lone a last a loved a long the") arises because words seem to have been split apart. The construction urges a reader to consider the respective effects of words split apart and words joined together (apart itself is a word of precisely paradoxical effect: like away, it suggests separation more powerfully when its two parts are joined than when, in "a part" and "a way," they are split.) So the very first pair in this series of last words brings into play questions of separation and joining that already preoccupy the speaker as she contemplates leaving the world of the living and joining the world of the dead. The series of indefinitely articled words seems to float solitudes outward, constantly displacing nouns; indeed, the missing noun, the lapse of subject, is the point of the deathbed's speech.

The trail of indefinitions leads not to a noun but to a definite article, and the thrust of all those "a"s toward a single and terminal "the" has the effect of nominalizing the "the." And since it is the nature of the "the" in general to posit something already existent, about to recur or go on, no part of speech could better register the idealist ambition, or transcendental *donnée*. To move from "a"s to "the" is to move as if from start to finish of a slurred alphabet; it furthermore suggests the very gesture of narration's trail of givens: starting with once upon *a* time and winding up with *the* end. Here in Joyce, the *z*-point of the gamut (the winding up in the sleeper's letters) never delivers its whole end-note: its *z* of "the" is singular, unlike a snorer's, and its period is not even suspended but absent.

To study this series is to admire its status as serial étude; like the William Carlos William poem in which the phrase "They taste good to her" is repeated three times but with different line breaks, and so educates us as to the different meanings of the same words when differently linked or broken, this Joyce series calls the reader's attention to the reader's own disposition to make meaningful units by bracketing or clustering groups of words. The line, read conventionally from left to right, tends to fall into units of two: "a way" and "a lone", alike, remind us of "away" and "alone", and we join what might otherwise have remained separated (as the speaker of this passage aims to rejoin her father in death). Thus when we reach the next two units ("a last" and "a loved") we are still inclining to join the severed parts; the effect is to call our attention to the potential of "a" to become a prefix, and to recall the double sense of the "a" as prefix (meaning "without" as well as "in", and "toward" as well as "not": remember amoral and aborning and abed). In the string of a-words we might expect on a deathbed, the last might well be *amen*; but amen, of course, is another case, coming from the Hebrew for "certainty," and from *aman*, to strengthen. In this Wakean thanatologue we are ultimately both without the men and without the amen, too.

Turning its attention to "a loved", then, the Joyce-disposed mind (having been swayed by "A way" and "a lone") turns the positive to the negative, and sees in the attachability of prefix not only the be-loved but the un-loved. As for "a last", a number of complex possibilities crop up. The phrase "at last" keeps coming to mind (but there is one t too few for it), and then the joining of words suggests "alas" (but there is one t too many for that); only for "atlas" is the number of letters right, the map and the strongman right at home in the topographies of this fevered speaker's mind.

When we move to the last unit ("a long the") we have to revise our reading-habits, for this one doesn't simply repeat the pattern (as "a long" would tidily—too tidily—have done, had it ended the book, recurring to the model of "a way" and "a lone"). The "the" after "a long" throws the unit-pattern off, and forces us to reconsider our clusterings. Thus we go back and begin to try clustering by threes (overlapping threes: "a lone a", "a last a", "a loved a"—cases where the second "a" becomes a kind of noun; and then "a long the", where the "the" becomes a noun). Between "a last a" and "a long the" is the word "loved", which can function as a verb and thus avoid, in one reading, the overlapping of units at the end, and result in a kind of sentence within the line (to the effect that "a long the" was loved by "a last a".) All the insecurity and multiplicity of the indefinite articles then yearn toward the singularity and security of the definite. If at the end of a line of life, the realm of death proposes the one surer thing, the lasting one, then the double sense of "last" (as adjective meaning "final" and as verb meaning "persist") is called into play, and the "long" (which is the lasting) succeeds the "last" (which is the longing).

When a reader has to regroup grammatical and syntactical elements within the line, and as the assumptions that underlie reading lead to instabilities requiring resumptions on different premises than before, no reading stays settled, and no conclusion can be unequivocally drawn. We cannot be sure whether we end in the destination of the definite article taken as noun, or the incompletion of the "the" as article without its noun, driving us back toward the insecure verb-name ("riverrun") with which the novel begins. In many ways, these considerations are all questions of boundary—where a noun becomes a verb and vice versa, how parts of speech are separable or joinable, where a line becomes a sentence, where a life spills over, what its period or end-stop is, and the themes of solitude and interpenetration which constitute the social meditations of the speaker as she lies dying. It's no accident that (unriven) the word "riverrun" contains its own *rive* or bank, its coursing's very boundary. For surely in a sense this last line (this death-line or life-line) is itself a short discourse on coursing, on cursives and currents of reading. Given "Given!

A way", we are given away: our habits of reading (habits of linkage and separation, clustering and isolating) are not unrelated to our habits of living, and in the exquisite etude of these eleven words, we are as readers in time both betrayed and shown a path.

*

The Course of a Particular

Today the leaves cry, hanging on branches swept by wind,
Yet the nothingness of winter becomes a little less.
It is still full of icy shades and shapen snow.

The leaves cry . . . One holds off and merely hears the cry.
It is a busy cry, concerning someone else.
And though one says that one is part of everything,

There is a conflict, there is a resistance involved;
And being part is an exertion that declines:
One feels the life of that which gives life as it is.

The leaves cry. It is not a cry of divine attention,
Nor the smoke-drift of puffed-out heroes, nor human cry.
It is the cry of leaves that do not transcend themselves,

In the absence of fantasia, without meaning more
Than they are in the final finding of the ear, in the thing
Itself, until, at last, the cry concerns no one at all.[27]

If you know Stevens, you can't read "The Course of a Particular" and not think of "The Snow Man" (". . . the listener, who listens in the snow / And, nothing himself, beholds / Nothing that is not there and the nothing that is"). Both poems require that we be present to nature without mis/ re-presenting it; both warn against the anthropomorphic impulse; both insist that we mistake nature if we think its cries resemble ours. (Even in the word "shapen" we feel the alien form of it: for our familiar is the word "misshapen," and we've lost the sense of its positive forebear.) For Stevens, nature's beauty is that of a glitterer without meaning; its consciousness is un(pre)occupied ("leaves . . . do not transcend themselves," leaves . . . don't mean "more / Than they are . . ."").

Where these leaves of nature do come (to mean something) is "in the . . . finding of the ear," which assertion seems at first to make the ear the findee of the cry's seeking and locating, but then, in the reader's changing mind, yields the ear as finder, as objective genitive gives way to subjective genitive. The object (the cry) enters the subject (the sentient ear is a thing made self); and can come and go until the fatal moment when self becomes an object (the dead ear, a self made into thing).

The being of the leaves isn't the leaves' concern, it's ours, just as our own being is; it exists in an ear, in a perceiving. Now occupied by what it hears, the listener's ear becomes "the thing itself"; "the thing itself" is the site of thing-becoming-self, as being bestows being on things around it. But things bestow thinghood on being, ultimately, too; and the poem's final clause ("until, at last, the cry concerns no one at all") sets the limit to the self-creating prospect. For the very consciousness that makes the ear able to turn object into subject is itself the register and site of mortality.

Leaves hanging on in winter are dead, their cry is the cry of no life we can know. The cry *has* no concern, but *is* our concern, until "the cry concerns no one at all," that is, until self has died or subject turned into object. Consciousness loses all its objects when it loses its one subject. The sound dies with one; and the "no one" of the last line thus recalls the "no one" in Bishop Berkeley's phenomenological query, the no one who hears the tree fall in the forest. "The thing itself" could be more self than thing only until self becomes nothing but thing. For precisely what is lacking, "in the sound of a few leaves" ("The Snow Man"), in the wind's inflexion, is reflexion; conscious, the self never lacks the apprehension of its own lacking. This apprehension is the capacity to "behold / . . . the nothing that is."

In "The Course of a Particular," the particular is a cry that concerns first "someone else" (because one cannot be part of everything); then, at last, "no one" (because at last one is not part of *any*thing). This progression, from not-being-a-part-of-everything, to not-being-a-part-of-anything, *is* the course of a particular. Had the last words been ". . . until, at last, *a* cry [instead of "the cry"] concerns no one at all" the effect would have been radically different. Not only the "cry" but the "no-one" would change. That is, we would, instead of the particular cry falling unresponded-to on the particular ear, have had *any* cry not concerning *any* one—a much broader, almost apocalyptic rendering. But Stevens's subtle evocation is of a self's increasing apartness, seen always from the difficult position inside a self. The course of a particular is deathward, but the course of generality is not. The distinction is crucial, and here it lies in the articles, more than in the nouns.

The River of Rivers in Connecticut

There is a great river this side of Stygia,
Before one comes to the first black cataracts
And trees that lack the intelligence of trees.

In that river, far this side of Stygia,
The mere flowing of the water is a gayety,
Flashing and flashing in the sun. On its banks,

No shadow walks. The river is fateful,
Like the last one. But there is no ferryman.
He could not bend against its propelling force.

It is not to be seen beneath the appearances
That tell of it. The steeple at Farmington
Stands glistening and Haddam shines and sways.

It is the third commonness with light and air,
A curriculum, a vigor, a local abstraction . . .
Call it, once more, a river, an unnamed flowing,

Space-filled, reflecting the seasons, the folk-lore
Of each of the senses; call it, again and again,
The river that flows nowhere, like a sea.[28]

The poem's title could pass for a passing epithet for God (a river is the one who rives or who divides); but the river's meaning, like the river's being, keeps turning, in the poem's course. In this poem, namings turn to callings. Running through the poem, a particular river (passing Farmington and Haddam, in locality, in Connecticut) runs toward abstraction. Out of a polarity of particular names—Connecticut and Stygia—grows an all-in-oneness that is the poetic ground. When Stevens writes "Call it, once more, a river, an unnamed flowing," all the elements—repetition, the indefinite article, the namelessness and unfixable site—tend to increase abstraction. In the last stanza even the river's content (water) has been turned to "space," retaining water's reflectivity, but mixing all times and all percepts. Significantly, the implicit promise of stanza 5 ("once more") has been overrun, so that "once more" is now replaced by "again and again," until the calling seems endless, and destination disappears ("the river that flows nowhere").

Here we reach the oddest articles in the poem. "Call it, again and again / *The* river that flows nowhere, *like a* sea" (italics mine). We might have expected "a river that flows nowhere like the sea," so the destination might conventionally stress the fixed and always pre-existing unity to which all currency streams. But the comma is crucial—it isn't flowing "nowhere like a sea," it is flowing "nowhere, like a sea." Here the sea is not the corral but the currency itself; it becomes one with the pluralities it usually unifies; and it's only one sea, among others.

In this poem there is no other life but flowing, and no other state but plurality. The usual contrast in dimension (between river and sea) is here relinquished (the "the" before "river" makes it relatively mythic, while the "a" before "sea" makes it relatively small). The conventional difference in motion is also de-emphasized; *both* flow, one in-and-out, one out-and-out. The usual drift of rivers is directional (thus time is evoked) but also destinational ("The river is fateful / Like the last one. But there is no ferryman"). Briefly, we read "the last one" to mean "the previous one" (the poem's coursing past reference points, linear as a construction of time, fools us into thinking so). But then a few words later we realize "the last one" means the last one TO BE: that is, the future one—the foregone one, the Styx.

This shift in readerly apprehension of time (from aiming back to aiming ahead) is itself an inscription of the shift from currential to tidal, and anticipates the turn to a sea at the end: the directionalities of seas are continually being undone, or balanced, by their tidal opposites.

The sense in which the sea goes nowhere is usually conceived as different from the sense in which a river does: a river goes to be lost by definition, in the sea; a river goes to where the other nowhere-goer comes and goes upon itself. "Call it once more a river" turns, in the last stanza, to "call it again and again / The river": the indefinite article of the penultimate stanza ("a river") has turned to the definite article of the ultimate ("the river").

One good turn remains; the sea's article is turned. The running to ends (the Stygia of destinations, the fatality of "[only] once more") becomes the circling of an endlessness ("again and again," to go "nowhere"). Proper naming (Connecticut, or Styx) turns to abstraction, flows into the indefinition of "a sea." The title's "river of rivers" undergoes a sea-change too, in the reader's course of mind; for at last it can no longer mean the *best* of all rivers, or *first* among rivers, epitome, but rather the river that *comprehends* other rivers. The self-distinguishing comes to be replaced by an other-comprehending "river of rivers": a river *full of* rivers—not one out of many, but one full of many. It is Stevens's astonishing achievement to have made the indefinite article the more capacious one, and in refusing ideal source or destination, in rejecting original or ultimate unity, to have come to regard the world under the aspect of an abstracting, but not a generalizing, eye. The poem "On the Road Home" aims for no Eden of metaphysical origin or unity, but rather for a nature freed from such perspectives:

> It was when I said,
> "There is no such thing as the truth,"
> That the grapes seemed fatter.
> The fox ran out of his hole.

> You . . . You said
> "There are many truths,
> But they are not parts of a truth."
> Then the tree, at night, began to change,
>
> Smoking through green and smoking blue.
> We were two figures in a wood.
> We said we stood alone . . .[29]

Without "the truth" or even "a truth" in totality, "we" can go back to change the meaning of the fall: "the tree . . . began to change" is not only a seasonal but a metaphysical adjustment; with no ground in truth for the knowledge of good and evil, we can eat from the tree without sinning, and truly be alone in nature.

This poem's road goes to the home of words, where in the beginning something was said, and it wasn't even true. We said we stood alone, but we said "we." Where was it, Stevens asks (in "The Man on the Dump"), "one first heard of the truth" (which ever since has troubled our ideation, and Platoed our ways)? Where did we get this idea of a real McQuoi, a genuine article?

"The the," says Stevens. Coming as they do after the question "Where was it one first heard of the truth?" those two words are either apposition or answer. If they serve as answer, then "the the" is where it all began: where something unique multiplies itself (and then claims to result in itself). The "the" is the only article that can do so: an "a" is never so replicating (when it articles its nominalized self, it changes its identity, and adds an n). The trouble of "the truth" is the trouble of "the the": as if to make a bigger singularity, it doubles up (it hurts itself) in the act of pronouncing itself.

But *one* is bigger, oddly enough, than *one one*. Freed from the dispositions of the truth, "the grapes seemed fatter." The tree (freed of idealism's stasis) begins to smoke, through its own colors and into the sky's (this is its life, a slow combustion). "Smoking through green and smoking blue": this play of transitive and intransitive smokings mixes object and subject in more ways than one, not least of all because it could all be in the beholder's (green or blue) eye. "The" truth generalizes its beholders' differences away. But "a" truth suffers change, and the fruit fallen into time (whether or not from the tree of knowledge) must attract a sensualist. The fox then almost overflows from his hole.

What Dickinson Makes
a Dash For

Interpretive Insecurity as Poetic Freedom

I

It is no accident that book, sentence, and pen are the terms not only of artistic profession, but of penal containment. Profession is, itself, a prison, unless or until it can say so (that is, investigate its own opposite—say, confession). The professor is trapped in the terms of his work, in the roots (i.e., ends) of terms themselves. Subject and object change places in the first person, and, as William James so mercilessly put it, "The natural enemy of any subject is the professor thereof." Emily Dickinson's fierceness in resistance to received readings is legendary; where the Sign takes on the burden of a preconception (de-conception, in Christianity) she finds herself having to use signs to fight its presumptive upper case.

> He preached upon "Breadth" till it argued him narrow—
> The Broad are too broad to define
> And of "Truth" till it proclaimed him a Liar—
> The Truth never flaunted a Sign— [30]

Quotation marks are signs of the kind I mean: in this poem, the preacher's insistent exegeses (his representations) are precisely not able to remark the True. The relations between words such as "preach" and "breadth" start generating resemblance-lines: to preach away breadth is, after all, a breach of spirit, whose speech is breath. In mistrust of (pre)ordination is Dickinson's enterprise grounded (or better, rocked). Church authority's prescription of origins and ends can only, like poetic convention, constrain a discoverer. "There's Ransom in a Voice," she writes (#1251), "but Silence is Infinity." In Dickinson's dashing (as in Nietzsche's) one senses the will to escape from the high-security prison, and its sentences.

There is always an other, one answers. But in Dickinson it is clear that the most profound other is very close to home: like Rilke, she is devoted to the otherness *of a self.* Like Marianne Moore's, her peculiarity is fashioned in assiduous craft, and her will to be peculiar saves her from conventional doings, from doing meaningless time. Dickinson's now-famous response to Higginson is a response to the ordinances of the ordinary, which flourish in the name of the Public. "Perhaps you smile at me," she wrote; "I could not stop for that—my Business is Circumference . . . Myself the only Kangaroo among the Beauty . . ."[31] Like Simone Weil or Meister Eckhart among Christian thinkers, she doesn't take the Gospel for gospel. (Could God be governed by human terms? The truth is unspeakable. But we are given to speak.)

II

One's deep dividedness, in language and about it, one's intuition of some fundamental untruth in saying (insofar as saying instrumentally limits its own reference), amounts to as profound a paradox for poetry as for spirituality, the paradox, indeed, of incarnation: act referring beyond itself, embodying its own opposite. In language, this means the attempt to mark the indefinable, the endless, the unsayable.

"By intuition, Mightiest Things / Assert themselves—and not by terms," writes Dickinson (#420). The term "terms" brings its etymological ends to bear, and insists on living's endlessness, not life's object or destination. A life-work like Dickinson's is unsettling just because it insists on this difficulty, and constantly explores its paradoxical claims. Not in "Contentment's quiet Suburb" or "Vicinity to Laws" does poetry reside, Dickinson insists: its "Location is Illocality."

Formalities professing to be Form are constantly admonished in Dickinson—most often by example. When she capitalizes something, she entitles it, acknowledges its status among the Upper Case; but her hierarchizing is idiosyncratic, not obedient. "The obloquies of etiquette are obsolete to Bliss." So strict a passion, so exacting a permission (not merely to ease or please!) is a choice unlikely to be loved or understood by others. (Not all of us could do it; how few of us do even what we can, with the passions and permissions we are given.) Dickinson's focus is relentless; the work is to strip one's consciousness, not load it up; having nothing, or contemplating nothing, one is better readied than in holding on to something. Fundamentalism's fundamental fix is on *idées*: it takes the animation out of the soul's encounter, and substitutes a saying; it makes logos a dead tree.

What dies in the letter of the law, dies in the spirit of the law. Think what has become of craft, of the meaning of the word art. The dictionary definitions include "cunning" and "sly trick"; under "craft" appear such synonyms as "guile" and "deceit." This is no minor semantic peculiarity; the "artful" and the "crafty" edge our ideas of the artistic enterprise toward the shallows of publicity; sophistication and sophistry share a root. The paint-by-numbers sense of craft, a craft of ease and foregone conclusions, the craft we float around in, on vacation's reflecting pool, meant to kill time—are precisely at odds with Dickinsonian art. With Dickinson, the craft's afloat, but in no security; if it were only to aim where it came from, it might as well be hogtied, dogtagged, dead-godded from the first: it won't move anyone. Dickinson rides a moving, loves the flux, and studies what dies. This is craft along lines of Frost's ice cube on a hot stove: a riding on its own sliding, a moving on its own disappearance. Dickinson herself unfoots the privileged premises of sacred speech:

> The time was scarce profaned, by speech—
> The symbol of a word
> Was needless, as at Sacrament,
> The Wardrobe of our Lord—

At any moment of revelation, the materials of passage must fall away . . . when the soul is fired, she says, "repudiate the forge." (#365) In Dickinson God isn't dead, God is death. And in the face of death, symbols of all kinds (words, garb, and even—as word is flesh—flesh itself) are finally superfluous, like clothing on a soul. In Dickinson's hands, there is the deft and tripled sense of "needless": useless, yes, and without need, yes; but also un-needled, unsewn, seamless—the paradoxical *construction* of a sacramental truth, in the body of language: it must be made of what can't be torn apart by spoilers and dividers, those who lot up spirit's trappings at the cross. A word is "authorized" by definition, and definition is radically invested in its ends. Dickinson is interested not in the end's *authority* but in its locus, where beginning is, and endlessness.

Science loves such mysteries, too, the edges where conversions occur, the Zeno-lines where limitlessness is incoiled in nature, Mandelbrot sets in which infinities are nested. A denotative restriction can install such a gestural structure, but only a reader can make it move. And a field of simultaneous opposites can unsettle the most limiting distinctions. Matter and/or mind, for example, which is to say, matter *as* mind— "whichever" (physicist David Bohm remarked) "we want to call it." The calling has got to be inquiring, not only answering; otherwise we won't, from certain mental fundamentalisms, ever be free.

III

The snake that winds around the tree in Eden is discursive. There, human innocence is not just innocence of evil; it is innocence of the *knowledge of good and evil*, innocence of the *distinction*. The serpent urges exegesis on us: internalize the distinction, he tempts; not until after that could he himself be distinguished from all that is good—or *the* all that is not. Out of singlemindedness's garden, out of origin's lyric moment, slouched forth in consequence millenia of argument.

God is neither good nor true, Meister Eckhart says (God being none of the things we can say about God); the truth, according to Lao Tse, cannot *be said*. It is the law of oppositions that hornswoggles us; it was the fruit of oppositions that condemned us. William Blake takes pains to keep the contrary inclusive, as negation cannot be.[32] This is why Blake is both so spiritual and so irreligious. Where argument arises between nature and imagination, and Blake writes "To the Eyes of the Man of Imagination, Nature is Imagination itself," he is reconceiving the premises of argument.[33]

The poetic act *can* contain in its field of impressions that which is NOT known, not denotable; and its frequencies, its activity, extend beyond its nominal limits. But the poetic act is not reflexion itself: for in self-consciousness's most paralyzing regresses, one senses the systemic penalties of stage feedback, knowing knowing itself to death. In the poetic act it is more a matter of knowing knowing itself *as* death; for in the poetics of self, one's prized difference from others is loosened, and one regards *oneself* in everything.

That's why Keats says of the "poetical character" that "it is not itself— it has no self—it is everything and nothing—It has no character—it enjoys light and shade; it lives in gusto, be it foul or fair, high or low, rich or poor, mean or elevated—. . . . What shocks the virtuous Philosopher, delights the camelion Poet . . . A Poet has no identity . . . When I am in a room with People . . . I am in a very little time annihilated . . ."[34] A self at once none and many must query the very premises of identity. Nomination proceeds, in the first place, by distinction; but we cannot engineer, with however many laws and mechanisms, exactitudes of distinction among, or even between, beings. We don't *have* our qualities; we *are* them, and share them. Life itself cannot be placed, however finely we discriminate the moments and *loci* of onsets and lapses; this is the ethical dilemma for a science of denomination in the age of bio-mechanism. At no point may "on" or "off" be simply switched. By the time we name either, it already took time; by the time we say it is, it was.

A self that does *not* imagine itself to be composed of selves, that is, to be composed of otherness (for it is the singleness and unity of a self that constitutes its sameness) is the presumptive self of daily life—more reflex than reflection. Of his friend Dilke, Keats complained that he "was a man who cannot feel he has a personal identity unless he has made up his mind about everything. The only means of strengthening one's intellect is to make up one's mind about nothing—to let the mind be a thoroughfare for all thoughts. Dilke will never come at a truth as long as he lives; because he is always *trying* at it." The famous negative-capability passage is worth another look, for its consonance with Dickinsonian insecurity: ". . . it struck me," Keats wrote, "what quality went to form a Man of Achievement in Literature . . . I mean Negative Capability, that is when man is capable of being in uncertainties, Mysteries, doubts, without any irritable reaching after fact & reason . . ."[35] The leap to Dickinson's "In insecurity to lie is joy's ensuring quality" is minimal, in metaphysics' metrics.

Of faith, it is the paradoxes and not the formalities that engage Dickinson; she gives no grounds for argument (only interpenetration) between physics and metaphysics, flesh and spirit, living and dying, humankind and God, love and love. Meaning can outleap the limits a short-sightedness would set on it; the denomination may suggest, but not contain, its value. Much of the critical response to Dickinson seems short-sighted in this regard. Who'd want to win, for example, taking either side in John Wain's argument (*Professing Poetry*) whether the poems grow from carnal or spiritual love, whether she addresses a biographer's choice of men she met, or Christ the Bridegroom? That she wove both loves together is so crucial to the poems as to annihilate argument. What reader of #1241 would want to choose, between the lilac incarnate in the flower of its name and the lilac tints (untouchable) of sky (whose seeds are stars)? The poet continues to insist on physics *as* metaphysics; she shifts the meaning of the spiritual toward the phenomenal:

> "Eye hath not seen" may possibly
> Be current with the Blind
> But let not Revelation
> By theses be detained—
>
> (1241)

In this poem's natural analysis, the "scientist of faith" begins a closeted research, head downbent while, overhead, the answering sky is alight. The bloom of revelation in nature *is* all we have of God, God not only human, nor to be kept in a name (the lilac linnaean), not to be *had*, in a word, (not this, not this)—but existing as the thou of the eye itself, the open sky.

R. P. Blackmur, whose title essay in the collection *Language as Gesture* gracefully establishes the very grounds (or altitudes) from which occasions of artwork might best be discerned, nevertheless goes on, an essay later, to treat Dickinson as trivially gifted, calling her art "a knack" unrealized into a larger achievement; she wrote poems, he says, the way other women knit or cook. Such patronizing cannot but recall the good Reverend (made hapless by history): Dickinson having written him to ask whether her verses "breathed" received an answer that could only demonstrate Higginson's limitations, not her own. Higginson felt called upon to apply his brisk critical professionality to what already exceeded him. Her answer to HIS answer rings as rare and reminding now as it did then: "I smile," she replied, "when you suggest that I delay 'to publish'— that [delay *or* publication] being foreign to my thought, as Firmament to Fin . . . If fame belonged to me I could not escape her . . . You think my gait 'spasmodic'—I am in danger—Sir—You think me 'uncontrolled'— I have no Tribunal . . . The sailor cannot see the North—but knows the Needle can . . ." This last sentence as effectively passes for humble (herself the blind sailor) as claims the greater ability (herself the seeing needle). Dickinson's magnetics has its life in death's force-field; fame and its professions have no power to move her.

> Fame is the one that does not stay—
> Its occupant must die
> Or out of sight of estimate
> Ascend incessantly—
> Or be that most insolvent thing
> A Lightning in the Germ—
> Electrical the embryo
> But we demand the Flame

(1475)

Here the body itself is identified with fame, and "estimate" with sight's evaluation. (Dickinson, herself, *did*, of course, ascend out of her assessor's sights.) And with what poise for turns! Look how the poem evolves, from death to embryo, inverting the body's chronology. Look how exactly the word "insolvent" turns the commercial to the chemical sense; how lightning leaps into the cell, becoming pure potential, turning us toward an intuition about time. (Before and after do not serve us here, they are bound up in the body's chronology and estimate; potential is persistent, an en-during.) The poem's last word adds a letter to its first, making of fame that extinguishable thing, the sign of energy's consumption, and display's expense. Fame's light, like mortality's, is self-consuming; potential's force is that of the realizable, not the realized, its radiance always an incipience.

To read Dickinson is to be reminded that the largest flash does not necessarily represent the greatest power, that form can be as rich in flux as in fixity, that craft is precisely NOT inert structure or coy connivance, but an energy outbounding its visible materials, and referring through every struction (in-, con-, de-, and decon-) to the uncontainable, that intuited spirit or gist or Geist we sense as living's ungraspable essential.

Eudora Welty says the writer's work is to detect the pattern beneath the given, a shape at once lyrical and mysterious and felt, which "is the form of the work . . . underway as you write and as you read."[36] (Writer and reader both do it, intuit the shape in the act, and their acts are by no means opposed.) The mysteries of meaning (at-once-still-and-moving, at-once-part-and-whole, at-once-read-and-written) obtain in literary as in spiritual realms. They resist logical codification because they sense, inside all diction, contradiction.

It is not the definable (delimitable), finally, that interests Dickinson; she is drawn precisely to that uneasier thing, what can't be said. The relative exhaustibility of a literary construction is one measure of its inadequacy to this truth; and Dickinson's sentences and lines often seem designed (in judicious ellipses, elisions, contractions, puns, and dashes) to afford the greatest possible number of simultaneous and yet mutually resistant readings. Where a lesser writer might try to comprehend the world by adding more and more words to his portrait of it, Dickinson *allows* for it, by framing in opposites or absents, directing us to what is irresoluble, or unsaid. Where the addition of a word would subtract even one of the cohabitant readings in a text, she leaves the sense unsteady and the word unadded. What critics sometimes lament as cryptic or obscure in her work proceeds, I think, from this characteristic reticence—a luxurious reticence, a reticence which sprouts and branches meaning in many directions, the way more exhaustive (less ambiguous) texts cannot. Her weakest poems are the most reducible; their surprises are cute. But her richest work is precisely what critics since Higginson have called "elusive," and its signature is the sign of the dash—that suspense of punctuation, that undecidability, which is not an indecision.

Dickinson uses the dash to avoid semantic mono-determination: a dash occurs where the more exclusive choice (of period or comma or colon or semicolon) would direct the sentence to a single end. Because her semantics are multiplicative her syn-tactics need to be flexible, especially at the junctures. The same dash may operate in one reading as a period or semicolon, distinguishing what precedes from what follows it; and in another, only a blink of an eye away (and existing all the while in the text) as a sign of resemblance instead, a colon, for instance. Only by suspending the power of the period (definer and difference-maker in the prose sentence) can Dickinson interweave phrases the way she does, release meaning from the sentence's exclusionary powers, and nudge the whole occasion toward that at-onceness (i.e. neither-nor-ness) which is her manifold temporality. Dickinson, to put us in mind of the timeless, gives us, in #406, no frame but phrase and poem-as-a-whole, no punctuation but the dash; in doing so, she unlocks the sentence in which lifeworks are so often conceptually framed:

> Some—Work for Immortality—
> The Chiefer part, for Time—
> He—Compensates—immediately—
> The former—Checks—on Fame—
>
> Slow Gold—but Everlasting—
> The Bullion of Today—
> Contrasted with the Currency
> Of Immortality—
>
> A Beggar—Here and There—
> Is gifted to discern
> Beyond the Broker's insight—
> One's—Money—One's—the Mine—

There is hardly a syntactical unit here that cannot be variously connected with the elements surrounding it: if you read "former" as an adjective modifying "checks," then "compensates" becomes transitive; but "checks" can function as a verb, and in that case the line in which it occurs can be conceived to end in an implicit period, or the verb "checks" can seem transitive, and "Gold" its object. "Slow Gold" can function as an appositive, either to "the former" (that is, to immortality), or "fame." These interpretive branchings, each of which determines which readings are likely at subsequent branchings (channeling for consistency), begin to resemble the alternative pathways of computer programs. What is amazing about them is both their zeroing in and their zeroing out; the readings made available tend to cancel each other, but the sum is an astonishing set of potentials, act of comprehensive design. In a sense, it is precisely de-Signing, insofar as the single exclusive Sign is the model for Christian metaphysics.

Because the dashes ensure no one grammatical relation to the exclusion of the others, the verbal values themselves have a volatility no other punctuation would permit. And because the elements (immortality/time, beggar/broker, slow/immediate, currency/immortality, everlasting/today) keep up a dialectical tension in the poem, the fluidity of relations among these elements results in the most extreme interpretive insecurity; a shifting between identity and opposition, depending which syntactical cluster the reader's attention privileges. When "Here and There" come together in the vicinity of the beggar, we are on the verge of the last line's co-terminousness: one and other (beggar and broker, self and self) identically designated, in two *one's*. The terms "Money" and "Mine" seem at once related and resistant to each other, as sign is to source. In Dickinson's orchestration of opposing pairs, each keeps being both.

Dickinson's virtuosity in this poem expresses itself in the extension and conversion of the broker's own verbal denominations. Part of the pleasure for the reader lies in the numbers game the poet plays, arriving at the last line's teasingly unsingular *one's* (possessive, at first glance; contractive, on second thought); but the energy of an equivocality infuses every turn in the poem, in exactingly permissive homonymal choices and word orders. Consider the various consequences for meaning, if "part" is taken for verb as well as noun; if "Checks" is understood as a verb, with any of three or four possible definitions; or if "Checks" is treated as the object of the verb "Compensates." Consider the various readings which result depending on whose insight (beggar's or broker's—or, for that matter, the poet's rather than either) we take the last line to hinge. Indeed, the way the poem is written, it permits all these perspectives, and more. Substance is, in one view, persistent and slow, spirit relatively evanescent (rooted like "Currency" in running), and in this case the deader value grounds the more volatile one; yet, in another view, equally validated by grammatical construction, today's values seem the more transient, in comparison with immortality's, and the "Currency" of immortality must then invoke a kind of presence that the temporal present cannot contain.

The last stanza is the virtuoso reversal of reversals. "Here and There" the beggar is "gifted," and in the economy of Dickinsonian values, the gift is "Beyond the Broker's." If we read the last line with sufficient multiplicity, it comprehends the broker's view, instead of only negating it. The two "one's" of the last line refer at once to the same one (oneself, both money and mine) and to opposing ones (this versus that, beggar's versus broker's). This inherence of two selves simultaneous with two opposites (the conflation, in other words, of self *with* other) is part of the complexity of this text's claim on us as readers.

Finally, time being the partner of money, the last line's paired nouns re-call the poem's opening ones: *money* is to *mine* as *fame* is to *immortality*. We are not entitled to overlook, in so brief and brilliant a construction, the fortune of words within words: "in" and "one" are at the heart of "mine" and "money," surrounded, respectively, by "me" and "my." A mine, re-member, is that hidden hold where value is rooted and from which the evidence of value is drawn. What the beggar is gifted to discern is also what both broker and beggar *are*; if one is oneself the money, oneself the mine, then one is *both* source and evidence of value. Dickinson doesn't assign only to the broker the stigma of the evidence, and reserve for the beggar alone the subtler value; the line reads beyond that simple polarity. The five words of this last line work so richly *because* they are so spare, and not *despite* that fact: add a qualifier anywhere, and you subtract a read-ing. Dickinson's art here is an art of austerity, generating riches, ringing change. In the very act of reading, we are made to adjust our presump-tions; the possessive "One's" shifts in our understanding to the copulative "One's," owning to being.

This discernment of Dickinson's, which trains itself on the less defin-able, less delimitable source, rather than on the ends or denomination of value, is the same discernment we saw at work in #1475 (where inex-haustible electrical potential is preferred to the more apparent and dous-able flame). This potential or source or spring is the same "source" Valéry speaks of as being at once absence and the endless source of presence. It is like the nothing that generates existences, in Hindu and Buddhist philosophies. Absence and presence create each other, in the brilliantly contrived four-line poem which follows, whose simplicity *is* its greatness. It generates currents and recurrencies of meaning by virtue of semantic insecurity; it shimmers with its own opposite, until opposites seem less alternative than coexistent.

> Not that he goes—we love him more
> Who led us while he stayed.
> Beyond earth's trafficking frontier,
> For what he moved, he made.

(1435)

The last line accomplishes the poem's *coup de force*; but the govern-ing oddity in this relatively dash-less example is the period after "stayed." One expects "for" (line 4) to operate in the sense of a conjunction, meaning "because" or "since" or "as." One does *not* expect it to figure in the expression "made for," because that is a colloquialism unlikely ever to be inverted, as here, so that the "for" precedes the "made." And yet the period after "stayed" asks us to read the last line *just* this way; he *made for* what he moved (that is, he moved *toward* what he had already made to move *away*; having moved us, he became moving too).

There is a tension between the present tense of *goes* and the past tense of *made for*, and the spatial relativity in this vision matches the temporal one: the three gestures of the poem, (to go, to stay, to move toward), are poised in careful relation to human temporal positions. He *made for* us in the deep past, *stayed* in the more immediate past, and *goes* in a present we either cannot love, or do deny. The sense of compulsion in "made," the sense of emotion in "moving," contribute richness to the readings.

Even over the evidence of the mid-poem period, there is a powerful inclination to read the poem in defiance of it; to take together the words "he stayed beyond earth's trafficking frontier," to understand "moved" and "made" as parallel verbs both having "what" for object, and to read "for" as a conjunction, avoiding the awkward gymnastics involved in reading a sundered "made for." One is tempted to say there are two primary readings—a *colloquially* primary reading, which resists the separation into two sentences, and a *grammatically* primary reading, which observes the authority of the period. The two readings are powerfully at odds, and propose, in Christian terms, mutually resistant exegeses. For the colloquial reading, a paraphrase might run like this: he doesn't leave because he never came; he led us while *staying beyond* the frontiers of change, remaining himself unmoved; he not only moved us, he made us too, and though he is not moved or made he cannot leave us because he never relinquished the divinity of distance. This is the iconoclastic reading—defying the conventions of Christianity as surely as it does the law of punctuation. It is in accord with Dickinson's letter to Mrs. Samuel Bowles on the death of Mr. Bowles, January 1878: "(Love) is easier than a Saviour—it does not stay on high and call us to its distance."

In the strictly grammatical reading, however, observing the period after "stayed," we have another version: he approached what he had moved, until he overcame the distance and became us; and he is loved precisely for having crossed the "trafficking frontier" to become human, precisely for having relinquished the invulnerability of the ideal. In this case, if he *made for* what he moved (moved toward what he made!), falling into the time and sphere of earthly life, then "not that he goes" can assert one of two things; either that, having come, he never left (was never again re-moved into remoter realms), or that, though he *may* leave, it is not for *that* we love him: we love him more for leading *while* he was among the led, love him for *being* what he led: a life. In either case, in this reading, our love attaches to the compromising of perfection, and not to perfection itself.

The exquisite bittersweetness of this poem derives from its oscillation between two views diametrically opposed—between Gods of love and loss, proof and reproof, presence and absence. If he doesn't make *for* us, at least he made us. If he isn't attracted to us (if indeed, in the sense we forge for love on earth—relative, moving, partial—he doesn't *love* us), still we love *him*, for *not* being like us, even in this regard (our love being flawed). The oldest arguments (theological and philosophical) are embodied in the poem's opposing possibilities; and the poem's power lies in presenting them as one wonder, not reduced to the impoverishment of either answer. The questions which spin out from their embedding in the poem's single act of complex proposition ARE its spiritual charge, and they are questions that guide us away from answerability. What do we love—what traffics with us or what will not? What changes like us or what does not? Once he moves into relative conjunction with us, once he comes to have a father (as *we* had to) does not motion become emotion? Does he make himself? Does he enter what he is greater than? Do we contain something greater than ourselves? Can the poem refer to the making and maker of poems? Is the poet contained in the text, as maker, mover? Goes and stayed, moved and made, object and subject, are polarities this poem's current binds together. Isn't this the richest paradox of Christianity—a God who is and isn't flesh, who is and isn't born like us, who does and does not die? When I read this poem I keep thinking of the Zen koan, two monks arguing about a flag. One says, "The flag is moving." The other says, "The wind is moving." The sixth patriarch (who always happens to be happening by, in Zen stories) tells them: "Not the wind, not the flag. Mind is moving."

An irreducibility, a winging out of bounds, defiance for conventional denomination, are what animates Dickinson's best work. Here the authority of the sentence lies in its commutability; semantic oscillation is the energy to her illuminations. The characteristic gesture is one of deft poetic simultaneity or conflation, rather than discursive alternity; opposites are textually simultaneous because co-terminous, so difference inheres in literal sameness, thanks to convertible linkages, versatile parts of speech, and other strategems. The reader's attention may take some time sorting noun from verb from adjective, *sound* from *sound* from *sound* (see "The sun kept setting, setting still"); but the text takes no such time: it sounds them all as one. As puns shift function in the reader's attention, shifts are triggered in the grammar of adjacencies, which must be permissive, not exclusive. As between us and the optical illusion (vis à vis vases and faces, for example), the difference between figure and ground keeps differing from itself. We can sometimes see only one relation at a time; but in a second second (a split second) we see *only* the other. Our sidedness (not the object's) grows, in time, to be the focus of the enterprise.

Dickinson's poems don't *argue* the coincidence of opposites; they embody that coincidence, in acts of poised equivocation. Here equivocation is the greater truth. A Dickinson text defies the simpler, more exclusive truth of dualism, and so must the reader's attention. It makes no sense to seek the *point* of such a poem; one's work as a reader is to hold the more-than-one (and often, more importantly, the more-than-two) in mind— to be of many minds. In this sense Dickinson's gift is the gift of broad-mindedness. Her "currencies" (destabilized insofar as they invoke every sense of the current: present, power, flow, and cash's own denominations) recall Blake's "energy." Freed from the constraints of exclusive meaning, freed *to* complexities of manifold meaning, we *are* what is meant, what is moved.

IV

The little poem which follows is a contemporary example of the kind of permissive construction I've been highlighting in Dickinson. The Bulgarian poet Blaga Dimitrova proposes, in the precise polarities of this poem's construction, the truth of an equivocality: to be two-faced is to be dishonest, but it is honest to be of two minds.

> I do not believe
> in my disbelief
>
> that my life was time awake
> between two dreams
>
> that I'll return to air
> the breath I took from air
>
> that I'll grasp the moment of death
> when my whole life was a moment [37]

The poem depends from its own first stanza on two threads—one of creed, and one of doubt. If we take the relative clauses (the "that" clauses) as dependent from the first line's negative belief, we get a reading opposite to that which results if we see them as dependent from the second line's positive disbelief. Here, as in Dickinson, polarities form fields not only between but within lines. Each stanza has an echo of the same-made-opposite: not to believe in one's disbelief is a doubt which amounts to faith. Two dreams frame a life-time; two airs give and receive the breath (expire is the word lurking just below this surface); and two moments, incommensurable in dimension, make the last stanza a temporal complexity: a future when something *was*, a temporal subversion like God's odd grammar in the Biblical declaration "Before Abraham was, I am." The perspective of this poem ("my life *was* time") is from a position in timelessness: and the *when* of the last line is subtly double: the moment of death enlarges to become a life-long time, and the future passes to the past before we have the time to grasp a present.

If living *is* dying, as the sages say, there is no way we can pursue spiritual or ontological truth without deepening the paradox. The self is otherest of all, is utterest and everest. "The universe," says J. B. S. Haldane, "is not only stranger than we suppose. It is stranger than we *can* suppose." Truth's value slips denomination; any assertion of truth must open up the assertion's opposite, so that what we do not know may be given room. It must allow for what is beyond particular authorial intentions (we can mean without meaning *to*, despite the perennial confusion of meaning with intention); and it must allow for what is beyond any one reader's capacities. It must permit what is not yet known to live in it; it must change over time, in time, through time, as time. "We do not know the time we lose— / The awful moment is"—so Dickinson writes, insisting on no noun to round out the predicate; "A firm appearance still inflates / The card — the chance — the friend — / The spectre of solidities / Whose substances are sand —" (#1106).

If by imagination one means the capacity to attend to what exists, what is there without the blinders of convention, habit, sight—then Emily Dickinson's imaginative capacity is, like Blake's, a capacity to contain contraries and maintain them in energetic oscillation, in a generative polarity, without negating or resolving any of them. Inside one household's solitude, how did a Dickinson leap to the edges of the numerable? How in so small a space, fit such comprehensivities?

And how do we (booked, sentenced, and penned with her) feel greatened or freed, instead of limited, by her work? Dickinson's God does not give directions, or dispense authority from on high, in a one-way stream; his coming-down is the same thing as her coming-up, and time's structural irreversibility loses its meaning ("For what he moved, he made"). Her relationship to her author is like ours to her: entering into the poem, we find ourselves in a world rich with interpretive choice and directions to move. Entering the poem, we enter not a small place, like the world of "publication" of which Higginson was the purveyor, but a place the ends of which in ourselves we cannot see; closest to home, the world is called a self.

In replying to Higginson, Dickinson refused to sign her name on the letter or any of the poems; she merely pencilled it on a card she hid in a smaller envelope inside the larger one. It wasn't herself she was out to make a name for, when she asked him, "Tell me what is true." Among Dickinson's gifts, the greatest is the gift of entitlement to the reader, who is freed from meaning as monolith, meaning in the narrow sense, existing already in advance as unambiguous law; with Dickinson the reader's freed into the meaning of the moving moment, meaning that incurs its own undoing. For identity *with* is not identity *as*; to love others *as* oneself, as if they actually were ourselves, is quite another matter from loving them as *much* as we love ourselves. For a self-love, like a self, has no amount.

The writer is a reader of irreducible texts, and it is Dickinson's generosity, in some of her sparest poems, to have given us more ways to read than any exegete could fit into a book. Whatever was cast is recast in the heat of the reader's presence, and the poem which was a motion in the author is a motion again in the reader. The incompletion figured in the dash—is life. By virtue of it, the sentence is pronounced as commuted (and commuted as pronounced).

Essay at Saying

Paul Celan

When I read Paul Celan, I read his translators; and I read his translators with a peculiar sense of sympathy: like them I am in the presence of an unforeknown language. Celan was himself a translator all his life (from and into German, French, Romanian, Russian, English). Asked once about bilingual poetry, he answered that it did not exist: each poetic act is unique, he said, not to be doubled. I know no German (the language in which most of his poems are written) yet I presume to understand him; as a poet, I sense his compounds and divides, can read his rhetoric, if not his native tongue. It is as patterns of attention (literary and spiritual) that the poems touch me in English translation.

The finer questions of fidelity that must plague any act of Celan translation I leave to specialists in the German language. There are challenges enough for me in the depth of English approximations available, the glowing-through of Celan's mind-motions in them, and the gaps and leaps and glances of his madness' method. Celan is one whose heart a no-personed God seems most to have battered.[38]

He was born Paul Antschel in Czernowitz, Romania, in 1920, the son of Jewish parents who spoke German; he grew up hearing also Yiddish, Hebrew, Romanian, and Russian. In 1938 he spent time in the Paris to which he would return, finally, to live. From the beginning this poet's relation to the native (the native construed as geographic and linguistic location) was unsettled. Talent and circumstances would very early turn his attention to the splits and multiplicities of thought and language, thought *in* language. Any self-definition he might have sought had to accommodate fundamentally shifting boundaries.

In June of 1940 Czernowitz was occupied by Soviet troops; in 1941 German and Romanian forces moved in, collecting Jews into ghettos. In the summer of 1942 his parents were interned in a concentration camp, where his father died of typhus and his mother was shot. Paul escaped arrest but was made to work lugging river debris and road rock. In 1944 Bukovina was annexed to the Ukraine; in 1945 he left for Bucharest, where he began translating Russian texts into Romanian under the name Celan, anagrammatically derived from Ancel.[39]

The elements of this history—river, rock, killed mother, lost mother-land, the constantly changed denominations of European nationhood—figured powerfully and repeatedly in the landscape of the poems he wrote ever after. In 1947 Celan defected to Vienna where his first book of poems was published. He settled a year later in Paris, took up the study and teaching of German literature, and married the graphic artist Gisele Lestrange; of their two children, one died in infancy. The death of this child is shadowed in several poems, but it is the death of Celan's mother that his work re-works again and again; it has its traces in all the collections. He writes, as all his commentators are quick to observe, in a mother tongue which is also, terribly, the murderer's tongue. In the last five years of his life, he was a man who wept over perceived slights, who turned more and more inward. Near the end, visitors described him as "a dark and isolated presence . . . who sat alone immersed in geology texts."[40]

*

The images of shells, stones, and husks recur across the entire Celanian oeuvre. Strata of mussel-shells form the limestone topography of his grounding landscape. In Kabbalistic mythology, Washburn points out, shells and shards contain the lights of a flawed Genesis; and *Lichtzwang* (Light-Force) is the title of one volume of Celan's poems. A reader, faced with thematic networks as variously interconnected as these, needs to be equipped with special capacities, associative and intuitive. One could say such a reader needs the gift, at such depths, of seeing in the dark.

For Celan is the poet of the mouth and eye that fill with dirt, after all the words and light; he can finally not settle for the old promises of illumination or prospects of transcendence. He himself repudiated the poetics

of metaphor,[41] and the later poems insist, to that extent, NOT on carry-
ing something across, not on getting somewhere (not, that is, on bearing
forth, or bearing on, or bearing out) but simply, rather, on bearing, itself.
This creation is a suffering.

In a speech in Darmstadt Celan said of language that though it was the
one thing that remained reachable and close amid the losses, "it had to
go through its own lack of answers, through terrifying silence, through
the thousand darknesses of murderous speech. It went through. It gave
me no words for what was happening, but went through it."[42] This is
what I mean by raising the root "to bear" from the suffix "phor": without
securities of light or crossing, without prefixes of phos- or meta-, Celan's
poems become simply phorescent.

*

Here is a very early and relatively accessible poem by Paul Celan. In
it, the reader is aided by an informing structure: unrhymed couplets in
which the discrepancy between first and second lines, in each stanza,
keeps splitting the unit. Syllabically, in the German original, the second
line (three out of five times) falls one count short of the first; and the
analogical tendencies of a structure of parallel end-stopped couplets keep
getting countermanded by internal resistances, so two vertical series of
statements (the series of first lines and the series of second lines) begin
to emerge as the more commanding structural control, overcoming the
horizontal disposition. The poem tends to shift toward adjacency without
analogy, sequence without consequence, nature uncoupled from cause . . .

> Aspen tree, your leaves glance white into the dark.
> My mother's hair was never white.
>
> Dandelion, so green is the Ukraine.
> My yellow-haired mother did not come home.
>
> Rain cloud, above the well do you hover?
> My quiet mother weeps for everyone.
>
> Round star, you wind the golden loop.
> My mother's heart was ripped by lead.
>
> Oaken door, who lifted you off your hinges?
> My gentle mother cannot return.[43]

Hamburger translates the German verb *kommen* (line 10) as "return."
I'd choose the literal "come in" because it keeps this last turn linked to

what I feel are significant time-space torques: something lifted *off* prevents something coming *in*: the shift in axes (vertical to horizontal, or vice versa) is characteristically Celanian. (It also seems to me preferable to retain the parallelism of lines 4 and 10, a lexical parallel strained by grammatical disparity: "did not come home" vs. "cannot come in.")

In German the first three natural entities (aspen tree, dandelion, and rain cloud) are compound nouns, while the last two (round star and oak door) are split into two words, distancing thing from quality. Since separation is very much to the point in the poem, that shift in address, from an addressee nominalized as compound to one nominalized as split-apart, is painfully exemplary. Aspen tree, dandelion field, rain cloud, round star: the series move outward in extent of space: quaker, flier of seed, shedder of drops, fixer of the untouchably distant. The first lines address nature personally, in the second person—not the mother, but natural forms themselves, for which the mother might once have been a figure, and which now are figures for her. But the fifth and last act of addressing ("Oaken door, who lifted you off your hinges?") turns transform*ing* nature to transform*ed* nature, nature turned to use, actor to acted upon. And the door is the divider between, and demarker of, inside and out, domesticated and wild. The door is the place where nature verges on the denaturer, or renaturer. The door is where things turn in or out, turn up. Addressed as a door, the tree is dead. Addressed as a substance (*of* oak), the tree (*an* oak) loses its nominal outline or presence; and even the oaken-thing-no-longer-a-tree is itself *not there*, having been "lifted off" what keeps it in place as a marker of distinctions. The hinges are the structure's hooks or quotes or "brisures." Here we're in Derridaen territory, the *brisure* being that joining place, that place where two brokennesses come together, of which he makes so much: the joint as breaking point. In heraldry, the *brisure* is where a subsidiary line breaks off from the principal line; in poems it is also where the line breaks. All of these have their bearing on Celan's project.[44]

In this case, with the door gone, the hinges, marks of separation and meeting, remain like quotes around a missing presence. *Eiche* (oak tree) is turned to *eichne* (oaken, made of oak); the made thing hinges on an absent origin (shades of poetry). Back and forth, the door is not only the locus of a motion (in and out of bounds, between before and after, between here and there, between then and then); it is, in this case, the locus of a motion GONE: what everything hinges on, without which, there is nothing. And with Celan we are without it.

If there is any high-spiritedness to be gleaned from the aspen's shivering, it is that white glance into the dark. But the anthropomorphic moment isn't matched in the spirits of the second line, where the human gesture isn't just negative, but negated. ("My mother's hair was never white.") The focus moves from a glance-that-could-see to hair-that-could-once-*be*-seen (from sighted nature to unseen mother). That color of hair is the flag of a condition, an age: for if the mother's hair was never white, it was never old. It never got its chance to glance as brightly as white does, in the dark. At the heartbreaking surface of things, we see how young the mother was, when she died.

The whole sense of missing counterpart (in the mother's lost looks) is linked neither, finally, to her eyes which could have glanced, nor to her blondness, which could gleam, but to the being she never had: her old age, her white-haired self. The truism that one cannot lose what one has not possessed is utterly defeated in Celan's painful relation to time: his mother lost precisely what she never had, she lost her future. And he forever lost her natural presence, that living relation in which one can now and then (briefly, daily, normally) forget one's loved ones. Now, he can never do that.

The yellow flower of stanza two stands out against the green of its homeland (after all, it wasn't part of the Ukraine when Celan was born there): another glancing against a darker ground, for the grounds of the *Heimat* or homeland (always being redefined) must inspire mixed feelings in an exile: not only he but it too shifts. There is no *terra firma*.

The dandelion's yellow stands out against such ground, but only when it flowers (before it flowers it too is green, and after it flowers it grows white and breaks apart—flies to new ground, new home, as seeds wing off to where they'll live). The mother can neither disappear as resemblance into her surroundings, nor fly off and find a home. No longer green, and never to be white, she shows up forever in arrested youth, unable to change in time. This is a reiteration of the unachieved maturity figured in stanza one, but it also rings a relation with the poem's last line ("My gentle mother cannot come in"). The "did not" of line four turns to the "cannot" of the end, choice turns to choicelessness, rage to sorrow. For the speaker is the one unrejoined, unreturned to, and the speaking is forged of interlockings and links that shimmer when they shift.

The implicit questions (what do we come to? what is to come? what are our sources and ends? our native ground? where do we go?) are figured again and again. Where is it the water-maker lingers, that raincloud in stanza three? Over the man-made water-place, the water-hole or wellspring. But if there is a well, why rain into a well? (Because it is empty?) Or does the cloud form, rather than arrive, in that position? Did well-water condense into cloud (shift in direction of intention)? Is there simply an affinity, water to water, an attraction? The question is, what does a weeper weep over? Only what *it has made*? (rain over well? mother over child? poet over poem? god over world?) The mother's figure in the stanza's second line proposes a likeness with the water-shedding cloud, but a contrast with the water's selectivity: *her* weeping is inclusive, not exclusive; she weeps over everyone, not only her son.

The pairs of first and second lines don't fall into a fixed pattern of relations. Where in the first couplet, the relation is one of opposition, the third pair seems (at first glance) to suggest relation (mother as weeper or rainmaker) but then the opposition hits us, and gets internalized in its second line (for she who was quiet now bewails millions). As a vanished presence she has become generalized, her particulars lost, her hair and heart now nowhere but in his mind's eye: like all emotional interiors in Celan, this one contains vast spaces.

This glancing hovering falling winding cloud-and-shine of the mother's hair, the natural weather of her presence, takes one more turn, at the highest figurative point in stanza four. "Round star, you wind the golden loop. / My mother's heart was ripped by lead." Here the star is scary and gorgeous at once, as befits celestial tokens. It winds a loop of gold: figure of fate, or maker of ornaments; somewhere in it a noose is noted. It is a ring, an omphalos, star-knot of David. In its figure, threads or lines are hooked to the heart in circles; but in this fourth couplet's second line, one of the aims strikes and deadens the center of the figure: tapestry turns trajectory, bastework blasted, all the poem's stitchwork of delicate linkages (from the seeing self outward, from an I toward the sky, following the poem's anti-gravitational sight-lines) suddenly comes to fall apart in this line. The weight that wounds the heart also sinks it.

After the inverse alchemy of stanza four, after the high golds turn to lead in the hurt heart, we come to stanza five's domain: the door. The door is neither nailed shut nor pried open but is, simply, gone. And who could have lifted it, that door of definitions, the demarker between in and out, between living and dead? It's not that the mother is LOCKED out. It's that there is no WAY out any more, either way. The question of commerce between his world and hers is obviated; the way to come and go (in temporal terms not only the infinitive but the future, the to-come itself, the to-be of the future as presence) is gone.

The door is the sign of a crossing, a way. Now it's away. (The relationship between "a way," the positive, and "away," the negative, resembles that between "a part," the positive, and "apart," the negative: paradoxically, it is the union of the words that effects the sense of separation.)

With the door lifted off its hinges, the very frame of hope is missing, lifted out of horizontality. The poem is itself also a kind of door, a passage turned vertical, the hinges around an evaporation, sign of an instrument resistant to definition. A poem is a model of lost place and lost time; it cannot replace its subject. It's no use (like a gone door). It is the place where nothing happens, and is deeply felt, a nothing the poet struggles with, a nothing he can't get out of his mind, a nothing that won't get the dead back into the world. The dead mother, being *in absentia*, cannot move at all, much less move back to him. And yet she runs and recurs throughout the poem: every nature addressed in the poem moves to and from her; she never leaves the cantor's mind.

*

Memory of France

Together with me recall: the sky of Paris, that giant autumn crocus . . .
We went shopping for hearts at the flower girl's booth:
they were blue and they opened up in water.
It began to rain in our room,
and our neighbor came in, Monsieur Le Songe, a lean little man.
We played cards, I lost the irises of my eyes;
you lent me your hair, I lost it, he struck us down.
He left by the door, the rain followed him out.
We were dead and were able to breathe.

(Hamburger tr.)

This poem turns nostalgia terrible: its Paris of purchasable hearts and flowers ("they were blue, and opened up in water") gets into the room itself, the rain of romances turning to the rain of a grim sub-realism. The neighbor at first promises escape: Monsieur Le Songe (Mr. Dreaming, always nearby, a little leaner than expected) arrives with a game of chance, a game in which they lose everything, down to their bodies, his irises (felicities of pun in English) and her hair. The lovers bet their bodies on the romance, and lose themselves, by parts. (The expression "to lose one's heart" lurks just under the surface).

The rain leaves with the dreaming (so the reader wonders whether it hadn't arrived with the dreaming, too), and then the last line strikes: "We were dead and were able to breathe." In this self-contradicting moment, the question of sequence plays its part: there is a relief at the same moment as a dreaded outcome. Were we perhaps dead all along, in those days, in Paris, but only now able to breathe after the dreaming parts depart? (Is to remember not, *always*, to live in an afterlife?) The mix of pleasure and pain in this poem's atmospheres (blue hearts, rained-in room, the Mr. Dreaming you gamble yourself and your lovers away to) seems characteristic of times when young romance comes to be corrected by realism. But the end keeps the question unsettled, for the poem's last line continues to operate under a question of aspect—how acute (how singulative) was this death's moment, or how chronic (how iterative)? Are we dead from the beginning, from the moment we're born? In this poem, what he remembers is a dismembering. Perhaps the nature of memory itself has to be reunderstood as an interment, rather than a disinterment, of parts.

Time, in its aspects, haunts these poems. Look at the one Celan calls "Corona":

Corona

Autumn eats its leaf out of my hand: we are friends.
From the nuts we shell time and we teach it to walk:
then time returns to the shell.

In the mirror it's Sunday,
in dream there is room for sleeping,
our mouths speak the truth.

My eye moves down to the sex of my loved one:
we look at each other,
we exchange dark words,
we love each other like poppy and recollection,
we sleep like wine in the conches,
like the sea in the moon's blood ray.

We stand by the window embracing, and people look up from the street:
it is time they knew!
It is time the stone made an effort to flower,
time unrest had a beating heart.
It is time it were time.

It is time.

                                                    (Hamburger tr.)

Among the temporal paradoxes that unfold in this poem is this one: the more he asserts that it is time things were moving (time unrest were turned into heartbeats—or heartbeats were turned to unrest), the stiller the poem gets, until the last insistence of "It is time" falls almost utterly out of time. For the stone *cannot* flower. (Similarly, the likes of the third stanza reinforce difference over identity.) As soon as you predicate, you replicate: declaring "then was then" is no mere tautology (Lichtenberg says "There are no synonyms"): the second time is always different; no two same events happen.

"In the mirror it's Sunday" establishes the beginning of a line of sight (sign of light) in this poem of in's: Sunday is in place; it is in *a* place (the mirror). Sunday informs the faced face. Once the location of time becomes the location of the poem, the prepositions "in" take over; "in dream there is . . . sleeping" (like "in the mirror it's Sunday") seems to locate the exterior world inside the interior one, so helps establish a kind of inside-out world, warped by the fluid dimensions of the sleeper's mind, and recalling Steinian kinds of phrasework in *Tender Buttons*, a text fundamentally concerned with our linguistic and conceptual investments in location, containment, contents. ("In the inside there is sleeping," she writes, "in the outside there is reddening, in the morning there is meaning, in the evening there is feeling.")

In Celan's "Corona" one thing after another turns *into* an other: autumn eats its own sign (the leaf). Fall is after all the time whose sign is its sign's consumption. The season seems a kind of animal, as the mirror's self is a kind of time; tame at our hand, autumn seems capable of eating time, fathering it, and being it (just as our lives themselves do). Then time returns to its shell, from which it can sometime come again.

And this begins the list of in-stances: the day in the mirror, the dream slept-in, in the head (there is enough room for sleeping inside the dream, room for the dream in the head, room for the head in the sleeping-room)—as in the in-framings of mirror on mirror, paradoxes of dimension lead to uncertainties of representation. All speech, meaning to mirror a world, speaks doubly.

To the list of in's is then added an implicit one: "the mouth speaks the truth" (i.e. the truth comes out of the mouth). One can take this truth to occur not only outside the dream, but within it (which is to say, within a kind of fiction); so the circles of interiority and emergency (insurance and insecurity) ring wider in each successive turn.

In the way the shell-house at the end of stanza one seemed to produce, as if by associative mechanism, stanza two's preoccupation with interiors, so too the mouth at the end of stanza two seems to produce the body-parts and -wholes of stanza three. Now the poem's plainly erotic domain is occasioned and entered: the eye moves to the sex, they regard each other (lover and lover, or lover and lovee), in a moment that can seem quite funny, depending on how synechdochically you see the regardee. (*Ça me regarde*, says Derrida somewhere, and means, in French, both "it concerns me" and "it looks at me.") Indeed, when Celan goes on to the next and parallel lines (we exchange dark words, we love each other like poppy and recollection, we sleep like wine in conches . . .) we *can* continue to read the "we" as being lovers in parts (lovers *as* parts) rather than lovers entire. In the partialities of this erotic passage, some surprising matches are made: "poppy and recollection" love each other in the nature of an opposition, for the narcotic undoes memory; and if wine sleeps at all, it does so by taking on the attributes it induces in human beings; the conch is almost a flesh-cup or ear: with wine in it, the human wit is flattered and waylaid.

By now the poem's trail of verbs has run from looking to speaking to loving to sleeping. Sea and sky and body's pumping all merge in the third stanza's last line ("like the sea in the moon's blood ray"). Here again we see a characteristic Celan gesture: a floating of scale or paradox of dimension: the sea can be contained in a ray if the small can contain the large. And the body's own tides are conjured up in "blood": the moon may be an animal itself (the ray) in networks of intoxicated artery. We don't know how far in or outside we are: both ray and sea may turn inside the human body's bed. The imagery deepens into imager and imagee, interiors which seem larger the deeper we go in.

The last stanza switches terms abruptly, as consummations will: from falling inward, the two burst out; from diving, they shoot up. There is the sudden will to widen the joy, publicize the private: it is time the outsiders knew the dimensions of the inside story! It is time the impossible happened, time the stone tried flowering, time unrest itself took heart, time time existed (for it doesn't, it doesn't) . . . It is time! Repeated, the declaration becomes subjunctive—time it were time—and the thing most insisted on slips farther off. Are the lovers dreaming now? Are lovers always dreaming? Subjunct, subcon, the roots merge; they are joined below . . . [45]

*

Sexual inroads and outbursts (dimensions transposable in Celan, as, often, in Rilke) similarly complicate the much later poem "When you lie in the bed . . .":

> WHEN YOU LIE in
> the bed of lost flag cloth,
> with blue-black syllables, in snow eyelash shade,
> through thought-
> showers
> the crane comes gliding, steely—
> you open to him.
>
> His bill ticks the hour for you
> into every mouth—in each hour,

with a red-hot rope, bell-rings a
millenium of silence,
unrespite and respite
mint each other to death,
the florins, the pennies
rain hard through your pores,
in
the shape of seconds
you fly there and bar
the doors yesterday and tomorrow,—phosphorescent,
like eternity teeth,
your one breast buds, and the other
breast buds too,
towards the graspings, under
the thrusts—: so densely,
so deeply
strewn
is the starry
crane-
seed.

(Hamburger tr.)

The poem starts from a fairly realistic locus. With some difficulty we can identify the bed of "lost flag cloth": locus of love and loneliness, the bed of mislaid banners, fallen allegiance, lost borders, lost belonging . . . Like Proust, Celan is interested more in the blur of time and space than in their definition. The poem is a chronicle of seconds split: the time when time dissolves each night: that time-place (in the wink of an eye, "in snow-eyelash-shade") where opposites meet. That is when the crane arrives, a kind of swan to his Leda, a sexual presence that ends the stanza.

But the beginning of the new stanza doesn't leave anything to rest; the crane becomes a time-piece as well as a bird-god. It counts out millenia by atoms (Celan's sliding scale again) and enters you (the poem's second person) in increments almost imperceptible individually but amounting together to a rain of dimensionless proportions: "through thought-showers" this figure comes to ring the extremes, smallest units verging on largest ones. A passage like "the pennies rain hard through your pores; in the shape of seconds" abuts the more expansive "you fly there and bar the doors yesterday and tomorrow—phosphorescent like eternity teeth." This shifting of scales is radical: time becomes money, money becomes molecules, between yesterday and tomorrow in the expanse of presence is liberated an eternity (but with teeth! as characteristic of watchworks as of lovers' smiles).

Something begins to bud in this welter of slippages, one into the other

(here again whole lovers are untellable from their parts), nipples, beat-
ings, thrusts. "So densely, / so deeply / strewn": the rhythm of line-breaks
quickens almost orgasmically; the poem's material dissolves into atoms,
and yet is viewed in such a perspective as to suggest whole milky ways in
the mind's eye, or the feel of flesh a mind reminds itself is made mostly of
space and the motion of electrons . . .

The last outburst is peristaltic, and seems to occur somewhere deeply
interior. Like Rilke, Celan sees no mutual exclusion between private and
universal: this climax is written in star-seed.

*

There is pain in the sexual throes of these poems, poems themselves
seeming to throb like bodily organs, mind-meat. Listen with the bones
of your head to the beat and speed; "In the bed of lost flag-cloth" comes
down in contractions, to single-word lines, to pump its star-seed out.
In "Cello entry from behind pain," the stanzas seem to amount to their
own rhythmic discharges. Each new stanza introduces a new vantage,
and the series strikes the reader first as disjunctive, then as metonymically
cumulative, until outermost and innermost seem simultaneous again:

> CELLO ENTRY
> from behind pain:
>
> the powers, graded
> towards counter-heavens,
> roll out indecipherable things
> in front of arrival runway and drive,
>
> the
> climbed evening
> is thick with lung-scrub,
>
> two
> smoke-clouds of breath
> dig in the book
> which the temple-din opened,
>
> something grows true,
>
> twelve times the
> beyond hit by arrows lights up,
>
> the black-
> blooded woman drinks
> the black-blooded man's semen,

all things are less than
they are,
all are more.[46]

To begin with, we might note the affinity between the words "cello" and *ciel* (French for sky), and the "entry" into the poet's name (the *cel* which came to begin his last name, after something—pain?—made him relocate it from Ancel's ending).[47] We are thus in a space of parts (of a shattered name) and partialities. Derrida likes to say, of the part that contains the whole, that it is "more AND less," not more OR less. "Cello entry," considered as a whole, as an arc from departure to arrival (the peculiar flight-trail poems make) is a score, virtually a musical notation for perceptual instrument, one which works through numbers toward a beyond, whose premises undo the horizontals and vectors of number-logic.

The essential junctures here have to do with instance, replication, and one-of-a-kind-ness. In spiritual journeys toward the beyond, Judeo-Christian constructions generally posit a shift in axis, from the daily linear progression of profane time or mundane time, to a vertical fall or ascent permitting approach to hell or heaven. In Celan, the beyond (hit twelve times by arrows) is not a beyond reached or achieved, but a betokened (or illuminated) one: in being aimed at, it is already hit by a vector of intention or direction. (Here we do well to remember the male sign has an arrow, the female sign a cross.)

But the *oneness* of the aimed-at godhead is its most *reiterated* quality (all the great gods claim it); and the video arcade hit (like the bombardier's) is, in its replicability, a kind of profanity, a joke. It lights up wonderfully and terribly; lights up to mark a success or devastation (it all depends where you stand, whether you'd call it sacrament or desecration).

And the sexual gesture which follows is also ambiguous. What, after all, is a black-blooded being? One full of desire's de-light, full of sexual storming, driven from within to seek another within? Or is black-bloodedness the sign of black-heartedness? Does the black-blooded pair threaten to reproduce its kind, or fail to (since it's oral sex)? Which is the better outcome, for human being as a whole? Is human being a whole? "Speak," Celan advised us, "but don't split the yes from the no."

The last stanza insists on doubleness (not doubled identity but matched difference), and explicitly so: all is less, and all is more, than *is* can say. Here, the "all" is the correlate of the "beyond" earlier in the poem. It has aspects both of less *and* more. All the things mentioned in the poem—act of sex, aim of arrows, breath over open book in the brain (for the temple can place the opened book in the head, and once again arrange the larger within the smaller world, the exterior inside the interior, the biverse skied with skull), the evening darkened as if by breath-bushes, the up and downgrades of approaches and departures by air, even the piece's opening, declaring itself in some senses as a score for violins (or violence)—all these are less and more than we took them for, because *each* is. Even the all that denotes totality (not sum), the all-comprehensive or all-containing whole that is *not* a lot of parts (the All, some might call it) cannot itself be denoted. No outline or verb of being can contain it, since it must include what is outside any outline. It is both more and less than we take it for, because the indicator arrows (meaning to mean) both diminish it if they hit it, or can never reach it anyway. Predication doesn't catch it, nor does post-dication: *in*dications cannot contain it. The quest for (or question of) quantity doesn't obtain, in all's case, or in nothing's.

Embedded in the German word for painting, *malen* (a word whose etymology suggests "to provide points or signs") is the numerical suffix -mal (meaning -time). Celan's form of representation is a kind of *malen*, not so much metaphorical as metonymical, arraying signs in time. It aims toward the out-of-time. (Sometimes to Celan it seems that death is in the past, birth in the future; but both times are borne forever in the present, which is no fixed referent but a motion.) Mind, with Celan, is not so much a computer of meanings (digitally registering yeses or noes, exclusive pulses) as it is a stream of emotional formings, deformings, re-formings. Celan's intellectuality is an emotional inscription. As Louise Glück writes, "a wound to the heart is also a wound to the mind."[48]

Celan suppresses the metaphorical tenor, in a sense; his evidences are all vehicle. It is why I call his work *phoristic*: the sign isn't separated from what he means, the sign (its motions and relations, its mergers and emergings) *is* what he means, is his only *means*. This is his sorrow and his strength. Absent in Celanian texts is the deliberately forged analogue-step, the similifying or metaphoring gesture so often taken (and mistaken) in Western poetry for poeticality itself. Between sex and death, matter and mind, flesh and spirit he erects no oppositions; and between the concrete and the abstract no sleights of likeness. The closest he comes to textbook poetic device is paradox. The poem "Haut Mal" ends "hallow / my phall"[49]: the spiritual economy here is deeply carnal, and the intellectual investment deeply ironic.

Look at the sexual pumping of "Cello entry," effected in the very language and cadences of the poem. Ones and twos, somes and alls mark the turns and attacks of the instrument. Note the first words of stanzas: in the original, *die, der, zwei, etwas, zwolfmal, die, alles*: the, the, two, something, twelfth, the, all. It is an accounting, or an effort to account. Like the

twelve-tone scale it marks an attempt to break out of the conventions of a
given counting or a given language pattern. (The graded powers toward
counter-heavens in the German suggest rungs, La Scala, ladders of scale.
In English we get only a hint of scale as subtext; but once we do get it, it
generates a great many applications: scale as attempt to go up and down,
scale as measure of relative dimension—sizing, more or less—the scale on
which things are weighed or found true; the scale that blinds the eye, or
falls from it, so that things light up or are dark . . .)

The work of poems is work in time. We pass through them on the
English page along two axes: left to right, and up to down (in aeronau-
tics, one of these axes is called translation). An opening like that of "Cello
entry" augurs further developments, and "from behind pain" spatializes
time (as do musical scores). The heavens and counter-heavens are traf-
ficked between, grade by grade, power by power. Airlane and runway
alike (line 6) are passages, to and fro. The evening is being "climbed,"
the breath "digs" in the book that the "din" has already opened—back
and forth, up and down the poem casts its lines. The true isn't a given,
it "grows" or "becomes," comes into being (it *wasn't*, once; it can befall
or arise, unlike the kinds of truths that ever were or ever shall be, world
without end). In "Cello entry" something shoots from here to there continually: the plane takes off, has a trajectory; the beyond is hit by arrows;
the man's semen enters the woman's throat; the woman is shot . . .

At a distance, something intimate is being done. Over and over, inside
a single human head, something far-reaching occurs. Something begins
by ending, or ends, again and again, at the outset.

*

"Die Posaunenstelle" (The Trumpet-Place) can be read in ways that
illuminate Celan's whole enterprise.

THE TRUMPET PART	The Trumpet-Place
deep in the glowing	deep in the glowing
lacuna	empty-text,
at lamp height	at torch-height,
in the time hole:	in the time-hole:
listen your way in	listen in
with your mouth.	with the mouth.
(Hamburger tr.)	(Ken Frieden tr.) [50]

Hamburger renders the first line or title more fruitfully, I think, than does
Frieden; for he chooses "The trumpet part" instead of "The trumpet-

place," reinforcing the sense of a musical score. On the other hand, later he turns "empty-text" into "lacuna" (a somewhat overspecific term that emphasizes only the break IN a text, not the emptiness OF one). And he uses "lamp height" instead of "torch-height," removing us somewhat from an available association with the torches that glimmer on Sinai when the shofar, or horn, sounds. Elements of the New Year service make their appearance in the poem, where we find recognizable Celanian features—directions and dimensions which incur simultaneous opposites. Deep-down and torch-high at once (out and in, at once) we listen with the voice. The position of seeker as speaker is, in general, the poet's position; it also frames the paradox of all spiritual quest, which requires demonstration and yet is, itself, the best evidence. What the Godhead (or Godhole) offers us *is* us: the indirect as direct object.

The celebration of the Jewish New Year involves the sounding of the shofar at a point of suspension in the liturgy; the time-hole is the inscription of a suspension. In his wonderful reading of this poem, Stéphane Moses cites Benjamin on Baudelaire: "Chronology, which imposes its regularity upon duration, cannot eliminate dissimilar, extraordinary fragments. To have combined the recognition of a quality with the measurement of quantity was the work of calendars, which, as it were, left blank spaces of recollection, in the form of holidays."[51] The New Year stops time in order to begin it anew. "At the heart of this interruption of time," writes Moses, "the poem's subject calls upon himself to listen . . . The text of the prayer cites the biblical text which describes the sounding of the shofar. As the quotation of a quotation, the sounding of the shofar has its place 'deep in the glowing / empty-text.' But although this sounding seems to be separated from the speaker by the unfathomable distance hollowed out by a double remove, it comes to him as the most immediate experience, as a palpable reality that inscribes itself directly on his body."[52] The horn itself has mouthpiece, trunk, bell (or ear) parts: the parts aren't only sonic but bodily, and are held in common with listeners who have their own mouths, ears, horns, and holes.

Celan's last line ("Listen in / with the mouth") recalls the attending-by-mouth at the close of "Cello entry"; and both lines present paradoxes (all is more and less than its being). The two poems' endings raise similar questions: are their terms generous or ungenerative? In such culminations, is time frustrated or fulfilled? An indecipherability of aims and ends is to the point, in such Celan terrains; can we locate the place of love or of holiness? Can place—or any of our languaged questions—obtain? Who is the lover and who the loved? Who listens and who speaks, in the mystery of such a seeking? (A profaner citation comes to mind: Chico Marx, caught in what lawyers call "criminal conversation," explained "I wasn't kissing her, I was whispering in her mouth.")

It is the poet's place, the throat. It is also the place where the woman at the end of "Cello entry" takes the man's shot, the target of sperm and arrows displaced from their usual sexual topos (in a similar displacement, elsewhere, Celan proposes that the chest should have eyes). At the end of "The trumpet part" the ear must yield its meaning to the mouth: of all these re-memberments, this last one seems the most obviously an *ars poetica*.

For "The trumpet part" investigates not only the attempt of devotion to locate its object, its god or sacred law, outside itself, and its failure to distinguish (in itself) that in from out; but also the similar attempt of poetic language, and of love, to so locate its subject/object, in text or time. The last stanza makes the act of speaking into an act of listening, makes the poetic moment itself, open-mouthed, all ears: in both is a powerful neither. In God's name difference is annihilated: God's name is unspeakable, unhearable. God's All wipes out the distinction of parts, wipes out the life of articulation. As Derrida remarks, it is not God's difference that places a sensibility like Celan's at such an intimate remove; what inspires such speechlessness and awe and sorrow, over against all logophilia, is God's *in*difference.

*

The great majority of Celan's poems are brief ones, especially in the later work, where his writing becomes most hermetic. Though we can imagine other forms of linguistic economy, though we have other models of extreme brevity and compression, Celan's seems radically distinct. In the aphorisms of a Lichtenberg, for example, the swirl of many considerations is distilled into one swift witticism, a condensation producing a precise and utterly economical turn of phrase: the small out of the all. (Lichtenberg's labors to reduce insight to *aperçu* are expressed in his own remark "The thought still has too much elbow-room in the expression; I have pointed with the end of a stick when I should have pointed with the tip of a needle."[53])

When by contrast we think of Gertrude Stein's "system to pointing" in a work like *Tender Buttons*, a hundred and twenty years later, we see immediately how differently premised are her points: "so then the order is that a white way of being round is something suggesting a pin and is it disappointing, it is not, it is so rudimentary to be analyzed and see a fine substance strangely, it is so earnest to have a green point not to red but to point again."[54] Here, the point of pointing is attached (at the hub) to a systematic way of seeing: a color wheel (itself, after all, a "white way of being round," in its sum). "Rudimentary" contains an etymological evocation of the primary color that green is about NOT to point to. The pun red/read figures elsewhere in *Tender Buttons* (as do other similar hints at the literary enterprise) so that the passage has bearing on that other sense of indication, the kind of system language makes, referring, pointing, according to a system. Stein is interested not in the pointer's exclusive refer*ent* but in its inclusive refer*ence*: "it points to point again." That is, meanings slip and change (it points, only to re-point elsewhere); but also, its act of indication indicates itself (it points to point, it points to indication as a sum of possibilities, not as a path to an end or way out). Now we are in the era of Celanian pointing. "Speak," wrote Celan, "but don't split the yes from the no." ("Speak, you also").

The Lichtenbergian (with its etymo-semiological footing on a mountain of light) is a system *of* pointing, not a system *to* pointing. There is a certain security in such a referential footing; one uses the indicator to get to the indicated, one follows the pointer, one sees the destination. The Celanian ground is a dark hole; the question of connection, of relation, is itself raised as boundless subject. The coin of Lichtenbergian economies is of prescribed or foredestined values: irony, logical progression, laws of condensation. The coin of Celanian silences makes an economy out of an atrocity, drawing our attention to the space where connectors are missing, to the cipher where one might have wanted (for conventional comfort) a deciphering.

His verbal pieces or parts suggest not so much horizontal logics as vertical relations (just as musical parts do). Forgoing the usual bonds, he suspends the meaning of individual words—meaning to be recovered by the reader in a charge of implications. (In contemporary physics, one discovers the invisible body in space by reading the motion-patterns visible bodies describe around it.)

Lichtenberg says derisively of some brands of brevity that "It is no great art to say something briefly when, like Tacitus, one has something to say; when one has nothing to say, however, and nonetheless writes a whole book (making a lie of the truth *ex nihilo nihil fit*)—that I call an achievement." Lichtenberg here is making fun of verbosity's vacuity. He is weighing up its poundage against his own and potent gramming (as the Spanish say, an ounce of mother is worth a ton of priest). But Celan really does want to give voice to a serious nothing, the Nothing or vacancy against which presence stands and is defined, the vacancy we face when we most fully occupy our lives—that is, when we press against life's limits, in space, in time. "Despite its frequent shadow of irony or detachment," writes Yves Bonnefoy of Celan's terseness, "nothing would be falser than to find in his ellipticism a desire to turn away, a will to laconicism, or a paralysis of discourse resulting from the evidence of brute things. The existential instant is what is signified by his brevity . . . the sorrow of not being able to speak . . . *praise be upon you, no one* . . . the extreme and finally efficient form of the desire to communicate."[55]

Where Lichtenberg is interested in economies of containment, and Stein in the stretched or warped vessel, its contours refigured, Celan's economy blasts open the container. It doesn't HOLD. Lichtenberg's point is clear, Celan's is nu-clear: instead of pointing with a pin (and pinning things to points) Celan looks into the vast expanses of space inside the pin, inside the atoms of the pin ("*endlessly making an end of things*," to quote Celan). He looks INTO the instruments of indication (that is to say, into words) and queries them. Meaning's conventional directionality (its pointer functions and uses) is suspended. I call his means phoristic (not to be confused with aphoristic) because he suppresses the tenor and takes the emptiness of the vehicle seriously (the poem is a haunting *machina* without a *deus*). Celanian economy keeps widening: "He speaks truly who speaks the shade" may say it all. It is not so much that Celan is out to contain the all as that he *provokes* the empty omnia with patterned shards or partialities. Where Lichtenberg makes a brevity *consequent* on an amplitude, Celan makes a brevity an amplitude must rise from. Lichtenberg brings an abundance or throng of *past* relations to a sharpened point of *presence*. Celan brings a brilliant range of *presence* out of a point of lost relation; from this point arise rich *futures*, in and to the reader. Lichtenberg spins in toward a security; Celan spins off from all security. If we were to hazard to reduce the two motions of poetic mind to diagram (which lies as much as other reductions), perhaps the respective gyres would look like this:

Lichtenbergian brevity   Celanian brevity

*

"I have experience," Kafka writes, "and I don't mean it jokingly when I say that it is a sea-sickness on terra firma. The essence of this sickness is such that you have forgotten the true name of things, and so in haste you overwhelm them with arbitrary names. Now quickly, quickly. But scarcely have you run away from them when already you have once again forgotten their names. The poplar in the fields which you have named 'the Tower of Babel'—for you didn't want to know it was a poplar—sways again namelessly, and you have to name it 'Noah in his cups.'"[56]

In a letter to Walter Benjamin, Gershom Scholem observed that the world depicted in Kafka's novels expresses "the Nothingness of Revelation." That void, says Laurence Rickels, constitutes the space in which modernity unfolds: "The Old Testament's double injunction to commemorate God without, however, naming him—that is, both to translate and not to translate God's name—finds reexpression in the Tower of Babel, the effort to find the true name of things, which is punished by dispersion and the necessity to translate."[57] This instability in the very grounds of language is, it seems to me, not only the condition but the content of Celan's poetry. The second splits: the split second is both absent and double. Celan stands there, on Zeno's ground: we can't tell its sands from its stars, its stars from its atoms. Something deeply unresolved in Celan refuses shallow comfort; the irresolvable is his ground. He can't escape the paradox: if he aims outward for spirit, or inward for a "beyond," the aim itself with its lines and hooks catches only *him*, in the act of seeking. Begin again, begin again, throbs the poem that cannot achieve (that is, make an end of) endlessness. Celan, like Beckett, makes, out of yearning and of painful knowledge, material evidence. (In what may be a rueful response to Blake's characterization of a tear as "an intellectual thing," Beckett calls tears "liquified brain.") That materialization of intellectual and emotional agony is the Celanian text: the beating heart is the beaten heart: like consciousness, all it has to pummel is itself.

"Mapesbury Road" comes late in the Celan oeuvre, and displays the wrenched rhythm, obscurities of meaning, oddities of means Celan is notorious for.

> Mapesbury Road
>
> The stillness waved
> at you from behind
> a black woman's gait.
>
> At her side
> the
> magnolia-houred halfclock

in front of a red
that elsewhere too looks for its meaning—
or nowhere perhaps.

The full
time-yard around
a lodged bullet, next to it, cerebrous.

The sharply-heavened courtyardy
gulps of co-air.

Don't adjourn yourself, you.

(Hamburger tr.)

One wants to place a world of silence, after such a writing. From the very start the poem seems to want to *place* things; but those places are securities immediately undermined: the first line's signalling turns out to be the *waving of a stillness.* And not until the third line do we realize the waving is taking place not behind the "you" but behind another person (a black—or maybe blacked-out—one). Our poetic grounding, our orientation vis-à-vis the "stillness" is immediately refined.

Stillness has waved in the black one's wake. It has made a wave in that space her moving leaves behind it. But this stillness, by virtue of its very motion, destabilizes the premises. The poem's next move seems an attempt to restore order; the speaker tries to locate time. Literalized by its adjacencies, at her side is a "halfclock": half obscured by her being? or by a magnolia whose blooms stud its face? or, as so often happens in Celan poems, are metonymy and metaphor inseparable, so that the plant is itself a kind of clock, with a halflife of blooms? "Speak, but don't split yes from no."

As for the red: unembodied, it becomes a substantive without a substance. What's the red *in*, what's it *of*? It "looks elsewhere" for its meaning; or looks nowhere, since that is where meaning may reside.[58] Besides, where it *looks* as if it were looking may not be what it could *see* (if it looks in the sense of seeing). "Looking" (specting) is itself a two-way channel: part aspect, part respect, it contains both object and subject in its potential semantic field. You'd have to see from inside the red to see where it is *facing*, in its own view. The questionability of categories like subject and object (their indistinguishability) is enacted in the reader/writer relationship always, but especially self-consciously in Celan.

The clock too faces something, but is looking—where? "Elsewhere too." Is the elsewhere of clocks the future or the past? "Or perhaps nowhere": (where else does time *head*?) The location of things and beings

(in space and time) becomes the poem's thread of theme and variation.
The second shortest line in the poem is "the full." The fullness turns out
to be (turns into, at the line-break's turning) the fullness of a time-place.
The scope of that time-place, unlike that of the halfclock, is comprehensive: "the full / time-yard" is individual consciousness itself, which seems
to surround all it considers, and even to contain what it misses. This
time-yard surrounds (here again the line break intervenes to charge the
moment of containment with a powerful vacancy) a small thing, but a
small thing that changes everything.

The small thing in this case (in this skull) is a point of painful information, a bullet. Its proximity (the word *daneben* means "nearby") points
up ironies of distance: literally *in* a brain, such a closeness is fatal; and
points up ironies of content (a bullet is not a thought). And the bullet is
"lodged," or fixed (unlike the best *idées*).

This new bit of information, this foreign body, this particular *part* of
the place, is really *deeply* out-of-place. Lodged in the time-place, this small
thing stops time: horrifyingly, the yard and time-measure the bullet is
lodged in are the brain of someone, another measurer's instrument and
sense of self. The bullet in the brain *means* something: no measuring (half-
empty or half-full) is going on any longer in *that* material. So the fullness
of that place is empty of meaning, empty of thought, full of matter only.

Whose are the "sharply-heavened courtyardy / gulps of co-air"? Is the
shot one not entirely dead? This would explain the "heavenly," the gulp.
Even so terminal an occasion as a death operates by no simple on-off
switch, no digital yes or no. One *is dying*; it's a process. Thus in the court-
yard which is the very field of consciousness, spikes of incursion enter the
perceptual area from the "other" side. The jagged breathing suggested
here is realized in the next line: the being-becoming-matter gulps, just as
matter-becoming-being did, at birth. The penultimate stanza is all gasps
and murdered milieu: what is co-air? Air you share with what's around
you? And what *is* around you? the world? Your idea of the world? Do you
live *in* your head?

One sees, one is seen. An other is nearby, and this other seems to be
dying or dead. One or the other addresses himself (for parts of oneself are
addressable as the second person): Don't adjourn yourself, you. By now
both reader and writer are implicated, in each position—as the one dying
and as the one observing. And one says to the other (is it I the reader,
saying it to him, the writer? is it he to me?) "Don't call it a day, don't
stop, don't go away." An I says it to a you. Don't leave the chambers (of
court: the court of mind, or courting of heart). Don't give up the body,
don't give up the ghost. Don't abandon co-breathing, don't give up the

being beside yourself. Being-beside-yourself is being in poems; the being-beside-yourself is your other self, your colleague, your co-spirit. With its peculiar lurches and withholdings, Celanian poetry is itself a co-gulping medium.

Love and death, their sometimes-similar incursions, spike the mental space and physical being of Celan's poem-breath. In another poem he writes: "An ear, ripped off, listens. / An eye, cut into strips, / does justice to it all."[59] No sooner does the speaker in "Mapesbury Road" utter the words "don't stop the co-breathing" than it stops: for his timing and breath *are* poems, and the poem ends.

The title of this poem is an address: Mapesbury Road. It is a place where people pass, a passage of message, and the poem proceeds by acts of location. Time is the space we pass in and out of, and pass in and out *as*: we are *its* record. At last the speaker tells himself (or someone) not to go out of time, not to forget. (For "adjourn" has its etymological time-marking built-in: *jour* is day in French, but *dies* is day in Latin). With Celan, one can't forget the words the culture grieves in.

The 1959 collection of his poems was called *Sprachgitter* (Joachim Neugroschel translated it *Speech-Grille*). Katharine Washburn says the neologistic title evokes "the barred window or grating through which the cloistered spoke to outsiders, language as a grid which filters the expression of ideas. For fishermen, the *Gitter* is a trap or net; in the physical sciences it denotes the lattice formation of the crystal. Barrier, net, grid, intricate action of time on stone or water, metaphor for breath which freezes when expelled from the mouth, Celan's over-determined word comprises a class of objects whose structures are defined by their relationship to negative space . . . through the interpenetration of silence or emptiness."[60] This is a catchwork of holes, a holework of parts—mouth, eye, ear, heart and soul. It is cast "down through the rapids of grief." Elsewhere Celan writes, addressing us as readers, perhaps, in part, "In the rivers north of the future / I cast out the net, which you / hesitantly, weight / with stone-written / shadows." For the speech-grid is marked in ins-and-outs of breath, life constantly lost, constantly *being* lost, constantly *lost being*.

Writing poems as long as he lived, Celan was keeping time. To do so was his *lieben und arbeiten*. He kept time, kept breathing, until, in Paris, in 1970, he drowned himself in the Seine. The river's name means "his" in German, and implies a missing—and feminine—noun. In French, the maternal breast itself is *sein*. Celan would have cherished such senses and associations. He would have known what "seine" is in English, too. For in English, of course, it's a net.[61]

Notes

1. The *Augenblick* (moment or instant) of the present slips from everything into nothing, in Derrida's discussion of Husserl's punctual and yet persistent Now: "As soon as we admit this continuity of the now and the not-now, perception and non-perception . . . of the Augenblick, non-presence and non-evidence are admitted into the blink of the instant. There is a duration to the blink, and it closes the eye." This presence, this that is going-on and yet is not-there, is the true subject of Capa's photographic diptych. See Jacques Derrida, *Speech and Phenomena and other essays on Husserl's Theory of Signs* (Evanston: Northwestern University Press, 1973).

2. Rilke, Rainer Maria, *New Poems 1907* and *New Poems 1908*, translated by Edward Snow (San Francisco: North Point Press, 1984 and 1987).

3. Capa, Robert, *Photographs of Robert Capa*, edited by Cornell Capa and Richard Whelan. (New York: Alfred A. Knopf, 1985).

4. de Man, Paul, *Allegories of Reading* (New Haven: Yale University Press, 1979).

5. Nietzsche, Friedrich, *The Gay Science*, #109, translated by Walter Kaufmann.

6. *Yoruba Poetry: An Anthology of Traditional Poems*, compiled and edited by Ulli Beier (Cambridge: Cambridge University Press, 1970).

7. Hans Kastorp in Thomas Mann's *The Magic Mountain* brings to his alpine "island" (he intended a short visit, but winds up staying years) a book he never finishes, called *Ocean Steamliners*.

8. All quotations from Valéry are from the *Collected Works of Paul Valéry* in the Bollingen Series, Vol. II: *Poems in the Rough*, translated by Hilary Corke,

edited by Jackson Matthews (Princeton University Press, 1970); Vol. VI: *Monsieur Teste*, translated with an introduction by Jackson Matthews. (Princeton University Press, 1973). Further references to volume and page are given parenthetically in the text. Occasionally I have modified the available translations.

9. All quotations from Aeschylus are from Lattimore's translation: *The Complete Greek Tragedies*, Vol. I, edited by David Grene and Richmond Lattimore. (Chicago: University of Chicago Press, 1953). Lattimore's choice of tense in English and his decision to foreground the question of forgetting seem to me warranted by Aeschylus's thematic insistence on the involved temporalities of memory, interpretation, and forgetting. (The Loeb Aeschylus has a similar version: "to those who know not, I've lost my memory.") The watchman's remark also draws attention to the economy of metaphor (plain and figurative, understandable, misunderstandable, and un-understandable language, etc.) in and about the Atreidaean house (Greek *oikonomia* is derived from *oikos*, house, and *nomos*, law.) To an English-speaking audience, the coincidence (house = house of Atreidae; house = audience) performs an ominous identification of subject and object: as coincidental addressee of the watchman's remark we are placed right from the beginning in the house where atrocity has been committed and is about to be committed again.

10. The vocabulary of the play (especially with regard to the attempts to engage Cassandra in dialogue) abounds in words destined to become key-notions in various attempts to deal with the tropological, attempts to define the properties of poetic language, from Aristotle to the Romantics and up to the present. Cassandra, in this sense, is a figure of metaphor.

11. Foucault's taxonomy of taxonomies is worth remembering. His book *Les Mots et les Choses* (in English it should have been *Words and Things* but became, at a publisher's insistence, *The Order of Things*) opens with a passage from Borges, quoting, in Borges's words, "a certain Chinese encyclopedia" in which it is written:

> animals are divided into: a) belonging to the Emperor, b) embalmed, c) tame, d) sucking pigs, e) sirens, f) fabulous, g) stray dogs, h) included in the present classification, i) frenzied, j) innumerable, k) drawn with a very fine camelhair brush, l) *et cetera*, m) having just broken the water pitcher, n) that from a long way off look like flies.

Consider, as Foucault does, what categorical oddities enter into this little text from—where? The Chinese encyclopedia? Borges? Perhaps it is most of all *our* text, the text that turns to our own apprehending, in which laughter arises because of the discrepancy between the text's underlying orders and those inscribed in our expectations, by custom and training. The unsaid premises of order ARE, after all, what make the SAID ones funny here . . . (Naturally one holds Borges, who foresaw our apprehendings, signally responsible.) "Innumerable" refers to what group of animals? A very large one? Larger than all the existent ones? Doesn't it haul in imagined ones? "That from a long way off look like flies" can comprehend, in a way, all animals. Certainly "tame" and "just having broken the water pitcher" are categories that could overlap. "Sirens" as an animal group feels disconcertingly close to the human category; the category *et cetera* does not come at the end of the list, so that what follows it is already included in it, just as the category "included in the present classification" operates as a kind of doubling from within: a representation of the whole but within a part (it is a kind of fractal factor). After citing Borges's taxonomy, Foucault goes on to quote a passage from Eusthenes. It runs like this:

> I am no longer hungry. Until tomorrow, safe from my saliva shall be all the following: Aspics, Acalephs, Acanthocephalates, Amoebocytes, Ammonites, Axolotls, Amblystomas, Aphislions, Anacondas, Ascarids, Amphisbaenas, Angleworms, Amphipods, Anaerobes, Annelids, Anthozoans . . .

Here I'll let Foucault's commentary speak for itself:

> . . . all these worms and snakes, all these creatures redolent of decay and slime are slithering, like the syllables which designate them, in Eusthenes' saliva: that is where they all have their common locus, like the famous umbrella and the sewing machine on the operating table; startling though their propinquity may be, it is nevertheless warranted by that *and*, by that *in*, by that *on* whose solidity provides proof of the possibility of juxtaposition. It was certainly improbable that arachnids, ammonites and annelids should one day mingle on Eusthenes' tongue, but after all, that welcoming and voracious mouth certainly provided them with a feasible lodging, a roof under which to co-exist.
>
> The monstrous quality that runs through Borges' enumeration consists, on the contrary, in the fact that common ground on which such meetings are possible has itself been destroyed. What is impossible is not the propinquity of the things listed, but the very site on which their propinquity would be possible. The animals "i) frenzied, j) innumerable, k) drawn with a very fine camelhair brush"—where could they ever meet, except in the immaterial sound of the voice pronouncing their enumeration, or on the page transcribing it? Where else could they be juxtaposed except in the non-place of language? Yet though language can spread them before us, it can do so only in an unthinkable space. The central category of animals "included in the present classification" . . . is indication enough that we shall never succeed in defining a stable relation of container to contained . . . if all the animals divided up here can be placed without exception into one of the divisions of the list, then aren't all the other divisions to be found in that one division too? And then again, in what space would that single, inclusive *division* have its existence? Absurdity destroys the *and* by making the *in* impossible . . . Borges adds no figure to the atlas of the impossible . . . he simply dispenses with the least obvious, but most compelling of necessities: he does away with the site, the mute ground upon which it is possible for entities to be juxtaposed . . . What has been removed is the famous "operating table" itself . . . I use that word "table" in two superimposed senses: the nickel-plated, rubbery table swathed in white, glittering beneath a glass sun devouring all shadow—the table where, for an instant, perhaps forever, the umbrella encounters the sewing-machine; and also a table, a *tabula*, that enables thought to operate upon the entities of our world, to put them in order, to divide them into classes, to group them according to names that designate their similarities and their differences . . .

At once Foucault has sorted out the texts' respective orders, and delved straight to the premises Borges so unsettled. Foucault does us the accessory favor of retrieving from the realm of the irrational the surreal conjunction on operating table of umbrella and sewing-machine: he reminds us of the *context* that can serve to bind a *text*—of the glaring artificial sun in the operating theater, that sun a sensate patient might well want umbrellas for; and of the sewings-up such surgeries as take place there may well entail. Sometimes a text appears irrational because its reason is too far underlying it, or too far outside it, for us to fathom; sometimes the text seems rational while undermining the premises of rationality (this is Borges's *modus operandi*). Foucault's reading of these texts, it seems to me, can help shed light on Valéry's characteristic gesture: a kind of cumulative description, piling impression on impression in uncommon orders, until those orders themselves become features of a new topos, the topos not of place but of *dis*placings. See *The Order of Things: An Archaeology of the Human Sciences* (New York: Random House, 1973).

12. There is in Thomas Mann's *Death in Venice* a related moment, an odd imaging up of the imager's own instrument. The novella concerns the dilapidation of the whole rocky institution of a man's life as a famous novelist—a story in which he steps out of his own life-story and examines it, sees then how narrowly he *saw* from inside his erstwhile "authority." The last scene in the novel, then, set on the beach, is *over*seen by an unprecedented apparatus: a camera on a tripod, but with no cameraman; it has been left on the beach, its black hood flapping in the wind where a head should be . . . This oddity, the surreality of the apparatus inexplicably abandoned, the device of looking *looked at* rather than *looked out through*—emblem of an art unmanned, art unauthorized by a presumptive "interior" sensibility, emblem of an instrument that works whether we *will* or not, attention welling up even where intention is missing—all of this bears the mark of modern- and post-modern-ism, lost faith in the priorities of consciousness, or seer or author, centerpiece.

13. Foucault's study of madness is a study of the ways in which societies and times have drawn that defining line around themselves, how they have institutionalized the *pagus* (whence "pagan") or pale—the line of trees, and what is beyond them. His is a study of how social difference is defined, how the "them" gets distinguished from the "us" in groups, how unacceptable differences are sorted from "acceptable" ones. Valéry's more persistent question is how we do this kind of demarcation within our own psyches. Where fall the borders of our individuality, our likeness? How far does the sameness we call self extend—the identity each one of us feels famous for? Valéry is always keeping a watchful eye on that I.

14. Martin Heidegger, *An Introduction to Metaphysics*, translated by Ralph Manheim (New Haven: Yale University Press, 1959), p. 95.

15. A point of oddity: *re*semblance proposes one of the few verbal cases where adding the prefix "re" results in a rapprochement, rather than a removal: resemblance seems to us truer than semblance!

16. The translations that I've seen tend to familiarize Cassandra's cry in ways that diminish its strangeness and force: Lattimore has "Oh shame upon the earth! Apollo! Apollo." The Loeb version is: "Woe, woe, woe, O Apollo, O Apollo." The Liddell-Scott dictionary explains the Greek "ototoi" as an "exclamation of pain and grief, ah! Woe!" At the end of Euripedes's *Trojan Women*, Hecuba, Cassandra's mother, utters a similar cry as she sees Troy go down in flames: "otototototoi."

17. *The Lyotard Reader*, edited by Andrew Benjamin (London: Basil Blackwell, 1989), p. 224.

18. Athenaeum fragment #24, quoted in Thomas McFarland's monumental

study of Romantic "diasparactive" forms, *Romanticism and the Forms of Ruin: Wordsworth, Coleridge, and Modalities of Fragmentation* (Princeton: Princeton University Press, 1981), p. 22 (translation modified).

19. Lyceum fragment #10. Friedrich Schlegel's *Lucinde and the Fragments*, translated with an introduction by Peter Firchow (Minneapolis: University of Minnesota Press, 1971).

20. My remarks on the ancients' fragments rely on the following sources: *Carmina: The Fragments of Archilochus*, translated by Guy Davenport (Berkeley: University of California Press, 1964); *Parmenides and Empedocles: The Fragments in Verse Translation*. Translated by Stanley Lombardo (San Francisco: Grey Fox Press, 1982); *Heraclitus. Fragments. A Text and Translation with Commentary* by T. M. Robinson (Toronto: University of Toronto Press, 1987).

21. See Jacques Derrida's description of the "hinge" in *Of Grammatology*, translated by Gayatri Chakravorty Spivak (Baltimore: The Johns Hopkins University Press, 1976), pp. 65–73. Derrida's "treatment" of Hegel's (and Genet's) remains, in *Glas*, ends on an unended fragment which might, itself, stand for Mallock's treatment by Phillips and Phillips's by the present writer: "What I had dreaded, naturally, already, republishes itself. Today, here, now, the debris of [debris de.]" *Glas*, English translation by John P. Leavey, Jr., and Richard Rand (Lincoln: University of Nebraska Press), 1986.

22. McFarland, as cited above. Most of the short quotes here I've borrowed from McFarland's very useful introduction, including the Haydon citation with which I've chosen to end this essay. I thus owe McFarland's scholarship a debt of thanks.

23. Louis Zukofsky, *Prepositions: The Collected Critical Essays* (Berkeley: University of California Press, 1981), p. 10. Zukofsky's lifetime interest in the articles is manifest in poems entitled "A" and "Poem beginning "The"." "A"–14 is the first of a series of poems beginning "An": "A"–15, then, begins "an hinny": and "A"–16 begins "an inequality"—so that what can't be reproduced is hinted at, yet an-hinny-quality is the hybrid that emerges. Zukofsky's trinity, "an, a, the" ("A" 18, p. 397) is fathered from the first, but it is only a ma short of arriving at anathema. Unlike "a," "the" is historically disposing, even "predatory", and thus (for Zukofsky) ideologically implicated. See Michele J. Leggott's *Reading Zukofsky's 80 Flowers* (Baltimore: The Johns Hopkins University Press, 1989), pp. 48–50.

24. Whenever language presumes to represent what is unique or unduplicable, its markers suffer this dilemma. Perhaps the exemplary case is that of God's name (in some wise traditions left unspeakable). "I am that I am" is an omen of a nomen: it is already doubling up like mad. Self-inscription always runs this risk: Donne sees it as the penalty of writing: "And I, which was two fools, do so grow three" remarks itself not only thrice, but more; for in stressing first the syllable "I," and then the spondee "two fools," and then, in a triple emphasis, the "so grow three," the metrics *re*-mark the semantics, so that the counting casts a solitude back on the first person singular pronoun: it comes to look like the number 1, first number in the series, and its loneliness is doubled (I am 1) in consequence of its triple foolishness.

25. Samuel Beckett, *Watt* (New York: Grove Press, 1959), p. 96.

26. "riverrun" in: *Post-structuralist Joyce: Essays from the French*, edited by Derek

Attridge and Danielle Ferrer, (Cambridge: Cambridge University Press, 1984).

27. Wallace Stevens, *Opus Posthumous* (New York: Knopf, 1957).

28. Wallace Stevens, *Collected Poems* (New York: Knopf, 1984).

29. Stevens, *Collected Poems*.

30. *The Complete Poems of Emily Dickinson*, edited by Thomas H. Johnson (Boston: Little, Brown and Company, 1960), #1208. All further quotations are from the same edition.

31. *Emily Dickinson: Selected Letters*, edited by Thomas H. Johnson (Cambridge: The Belknap Press of Harvard University Press, 1971), p. 176.

32. "Blake made in Milton and Jerusalem an important distinction between 'contraries' and 'negations,' which is the basis for his un-Hegelian dialectic. A negation is a situation in which, in an opposition like soul/body or good/evil, one side is privileged over the other, that is, one side negates the reality or authority of the other, attempting to suppress it. . . . Blake's example in the Marriage [of Heaven and Hell] . . . is the opposition soul/body: in the history of religion the soul has negated the body, connecting it with evil. This is a process that developed from original visionary acts toward priesthood, which bureaucratizes the interpretation of the act into law." Hazard Adams, *Philosophy of the Literary Symbolic* (Tallahassee: Florida State University Press, 1983), pp. 6–7.

33. Letter to Trusler, August 23, 1799. *The Complete Poetry and Prose of William Blake*, edited by David V. Erdman (New York: Anchor Books, 1982), p. 702.

34. John Keats, Letter to Woodhouse, Oct. 27, 1818.

35. John Keats, Letter to George and Tom Keats, Dec. 21–24, 1817.

36. Eudora Welty, *The Eye of the Story* (New York: Random House, 1979).

37. *Because the Sea is Black: Poems of Blaga Dimitrova*, selected and translated by Niko Boris and Heather McHugh (Middletown: Wesleyan University Press, 1989).

38. The following selections are available in English: *Poems of Paul Celan*, translated with an introduction by Michael Hamburger (New York: Persea Books, 1988). *Paul Celan: 65 Poems*. translated by Brian Lynch and Peter Jankowsky (Dublin: Raven Arts Press, 1985). *Paul Celan: Last Poems*, translated by Katharine Washburn and Margret Guillemin (San Francisco: North Point Press, 1986). To the above, and especially to Hamburger and Washburn, I owe an admirer's debt of quotation and paraphrase.

As Hamburger observes, Celan's earlier verse is less difficult than his later; what early on was understandable in his "progression of imagery rather than of argument" came to seem more and more obscure in later poems, even to literati. Like Gertrude Stein in "Tender Buttons," Celan reconstructs a reader's habits of association and patterning over the course of a collection's reading; he makes the act of collection itself (and its status in time, for a reader) part of the point.

The later Celan "begins to coin new words, especially compound words, and to divide other words into their component syllables, each of which acquires new weight. The process of condensation and distillation is carried farther in the subsequent collections. Both verse lines and whole poems tend to be shorter and shorter." (Hamburger, p. 23) Hamburger testifies to the difficulties of translation, pointing out how puzzling are the innovations that abound in the later books. Take, for example, this short poem "Once":

ONCE
I heard him,
he was washing the world,
unseen, nightlong,
real.

One and Infinite,
annihilated,
ied.

Light was. Salvation.

First, a note on the poem. It was the washing, not the creating, that made the light. Whether or not you add to the formulation of the "once" the specific sense of the "and for all," depends on how you view the absolutes of narrative; it is, in any case, the "once" that makes the glow of divinity. It was a restoration, not an initiation, from the first, that made the finish. (For a far-reaching meditation on once-ness and dates in Celan, see Derrida's "Shibboleth," in *Midrash and Literature*, edited by Geoffrey Hartman and Sanford Budick [New Haven: Yale University Press, 1986.])

Here is Hamburger's own account of the translation difficulties:
The German word corresponding to "ied" is "ichten." Since it comes after "vernichtet" (annihilated) it could be the infinitive of a verb that is the positive counterpart of annihilate, and that is how it was construed by a reviewer for the *Times Literary Supplement*, who translated it as "ihilate." This new verb would not be more far-fetched than other neologisms of Celan's, since in the middle High German, which he knew, there was a positive "iht" (ought) corresponding to the negative "niht" (nought). My authority for "ied" is Paul Celan himself. When I last met him, in April 1968, he was convinced that I was the author of the anonymous *TLS* review and would not accept my repeated denial. He explained that "ichten" was formed from the personal pronoun "ich," so that it was the third person plural of the imperfect tense of a verb "ichen" (to i). (Hamburger, pp. 25–26)

As the reader of Hamburger's bilingual edition can see, however, Celan's mind doesn't work with stable nuclei of meaning (etymological meaning included); rather, he proceeds by the letter, and because of that, even Hamburger's bold and ingenious "annihilated, / ied. / Light" must fall short of Celan's "vernICHtet, / ICHTen. / LICHT."

One reason why Celan "had to make a new language for himself, a language at once probing and groping, critical and innovative; and why the richer his verbal and formal resources grew, the more strictly he confined them," according to Hamburger, is that Celan's "German could not and must not be the German of the destroyers" (Hamburger, p. 27). Volume 8/9 of *Acts: A journal of New Writing* (San Francisco, 1988), entitled *Translating Tradition: Paul Celan in France*, edited by Benjamin Hollander, contains very interesting essays and materials on the problem of translating Celan as well as on Celan's own renditions of well-known English poems.

39. In her excellent Introduction to *Paul Celan: Last Poems*, Katharine Washburn figures that as an amateur botanist Celan must have known of the herb

celandine, said to cure weak sight; and that as a student of fourteenth-century Romance philology he must have liked the shadow of reference to Thomas of Celano, author of *Dies Irae*.

40. Washburn, as cited above.

41. Cf., for example, the short poem "A RUMBLING: truth / itself has appeared / among humankind / in the very thick of their / flurrying metaphors" (Hamburger, pp. 262–63).

42. Paul Celan, *Collected Prose* ("The Meridian Speech"), translated by Rosmarie Waldrop (Manchester: Carcanet, 1986).

43. Hamburger translation. The German original contains a few archaic poeticisms.

44. In his discussion of the *brisure* as "spacing," Derrida draws special attention to the dislocations of time and "the alterity of a past that never was and can never be lived in the originary or modified form of presence." (*Of Grammatology*, p. 70; see note 44. See also his "Shibboleth.") Paul Celan is the preeminent poet of this alterity of time lost.

45. To appreciate the poem's poetological significance—how it rewrites the topoi of the seasonal (autumnal) lyric, what it does to a repertoire of tropes derived from nature and the repository of a nostalgic desire for natural language—compare "Corona" to Rilke's "Autumn Day."

46. Hamburger translation. In order to emphasize the literal austerity of the original, I've modified his rendition of the last stanza. The reader of this extremely dense poem should also consult the Lynch-Jankowsky version.

47. I owe this observation to Niko Boris McHugh.

48. Louise Glück, "The Untrustworthy Speaker," *Ararat* (New York: Ecco, 1990). See also Derrida's reflections on poem-dating, wounds, and the translations of what in Celan is read to the quick ("Wundgelesenes"), in "Shibboleth."

49. Lynch-Jankowsky translation. The original reads: "du beheiligst / mein Glied," which Niko Boris and I render as "deify my dick."

50. Frieden is the translator of Stephane Moses' essay "Patterns of Negativity in Paul Celan's 'The Trumpet-Place'" (in: *Languages of the Unsayable*, edited by Sanford Budick and Wolfgang Iser (New York: Columbia University Press, 1989), on which I draw below. Appropriately, perhaps, the volume doesn't tell which language the poem was translated from, German or French.

51. Stéphane Moses, p. 218.

52. Moses, p. 220.

53. G. C. Lichtenberg, *Aphorisms*, translated by R. J. Hollingdale (New York and London: Penguin, 1990).

54. Gertrude Stein, *Tender Buttons*.

55. Yves Bonnefoy in *Translating Tradition*. See note 38.

56. Laurence Rickels, "Kafka and the Aero-Trace," in *Kafka and the Contemporary Critical Performance*, edited by Alan Udoff (Bloomington: Indiana University Press, 1987).

57. Ibid.

58. Compare Dickinson's #258:

> Heavenly Hurt, it gives us—
> We can find no scar,
> But internal difference
> Where the meanings, are—

In Celan's "Cello entry" and in "Mapesbury Road," one senses a most un-heavenly hurt, and holes where the meanings might have been.

59. "WHITE GREY," Lynch-Jankowsky translation.

60. Katharine Washburn, Introduction.

61. Consider the following excerpt from the last of Celan's posthumously published poems (*Zeitgehöft*):

DAS FREMDE	FOREIGN THINGS	OTHERNESS
hat uns im Netz . . .	ensnare us . . .	has netted us . . .
Celan	Washburn (p. 195)	Niko Boris trans.

Once we're acquainted with Celan's life-work of apprehended past, and death-work of en-seining, it's hard to shake the impression that this very late poem was written, in exquisite anachronism, as a footnote to a future he forecast.

Acknowledgments

Excerpts from the book WATT by Samuel Beckett copyright © 1953 by Samuel Beckett used with the permission of Grove/Atlantic Monthly Press. To order please call 800-937-5557.

Selections from *Yoruba Poetry*, compiled and edited by Ulli Beier, reprinted by permission of Ulli Beier and Cambridge University Press, copyright 1970.

The Robert Capa diptych, "Tour de France, Pleyben, Brittany, July 1939," is reprinted by permission of Magnum Photos, Inc.

Carmina Archilochi: The Fragments of Archilocos, translated and edited by Guy Davenport, © 1964 by The Regents of the University of California, used by permission of the University of California Press.

Excerpts from the poetry of Emily Dickinson reprinted by permission of the publishers and the Trustees of Amherst College from *The Poems of Emily Dickinson*, Thomas H. Johnson, ed., Cambridge, Mass.: The Belknap Press of Harvard University Press, Copyright 1951, 1955, 1979, 1983 by the President and Fellows of Harvard College.

Selections from *Poems of Paul Celan* translated by Michael Hamburger. Copyright © 1972, 1980, 1988 by Michael Hamburger. Reprinted by permission of Persea Books, Inc.

Excerpts from *Parmenides and Empedocles: The Fragments in Verse*, translation by Stanley Lombardo, reprinted by permission of Grey Fox Press, copyright 1982.

"A Genuine Article," by Heather McHugh, has appeared in a recent issue of *ZYZZYVA* magazine.

"A Stranger's Way of Looking" and "What Dickinson Makes a Dash For," by Heather McHugh, first appeared in *American Poetry Review*.

Pages from *A Humument* by Tom Phillips reproduced by permission of Thames and Hudson, copyright 1987 by Tom Phillips.

Selections from *New Poems 1907* and *New Poems 1908* by Rainer Maria Rilke, translated by Edward Snow, published by North Point Press, copyright 1984 and 1987 by Edward Snow, reprinted by permission of North Point Press and Edward Snow.

"On the Road Home" by Wallace Stevens is reprinted by permission of Alfred A. Knopf, Inc. from *Collected Poems*, copyright 1942 by Wallace Stevens and renewed 1970 by Holly Stevens.

"The River of Rivers in Connecticut" by Wallace Stevens is reprinted by permission of Alfred A. Knopf, Inc., from *Collected Poems*, copyright 1954 by Wallace Stevens.

"The Course of a Particular" by Wallace Stevens is reprinted from *Opus Posthumous* by Wallace Stevens. Copyright 1957 by Elsie Stevens and Holly Stevens. Reprinted by permission of Alfred A. Knopf, Inc.

Excerpts from Valéry, Paul, *The Collected Works: Monsieur Teste* (Vol. VI) and *Poems in the Rough* (Vol. II). Copyright © 1970 by Princeton University Press. Reprinted by permission of Princeton University Press.

Index of Names

UNIVERSITY PRESS OF NEW ENGLAND
publishes books under its own imprint and is the
publisher for Brandeis University Press, Brown
University Press, University of Connecticut,
Dartmouth College, Middlebury College Press,
University of New Hampshire, University of
Rhode Island, Tufts University, University of
Vermont, and Wesleyan University Press.

HEATHER McHUGH
is Professor of English at the University of
Washington. She has published four books of poetry
and two of translation; her most recent collections
are *Shades* [1988] and *To the Quick* [1987].

LIBRARY OF CONGRESS CATALOGING-IN-
PUBLICATION DATA
McHugh, Heather, 1948–
    Broken English : poetry and partiality / Heather McHugh.
        p.   cm.
    Includes index.
    ISBN 0–8195–5268–2. — ISBN 0–8195–6272–6 (pbk.)
    1. McHugh, Heather, 1948–   —Aesthetics.
    2. Literature—History and criticism—Theory, etc.
    3. Poetry.   I. Title.
    PS3563.A311614B76   1993
    809.1—dc20   93–13612
    ∞